I0456181

1

HUMAN AND

ECONOMIC

GEOGRAPHY

WRITEN BY:
FRANK PHILEMON
P.O. BOX 116,
LIWALE-LINDI.
TANZANIA
TEL: +255762426746/+255683114202.
EMAIL: naxfra@gmail.com

All rights reserved. No part of this publication may be reproduced, stored in retrieval system, photocopying, recording or transmitted in any means, including electronics, magnetic, or otherwise, without prior written permission from the author.
Copyright © 2016

HUMAN AND ECONOMIC GEOGRAPHY

MWL. FRANK PHILEMON

PREFACE

Several studies and researches are undertaken and accomplished year after year and in the most cases, much attention is paid to an important dimension relating to Geography. This book will contain particularly Human and Economic Geography approaches and too many trial questions. The need therefore, is for those concerned with geography to pay attention to designing and adhering to the appropriate intensive reading for improving their understanding.

This book has been written with the aim of helping Geographers; learners, facilitators and others who are interested in geography phenomena in developing appropriate skills for their geography studies and works as well as making them familiar with the art of using different methods and techniques in Human and Economic Geography. Geographical aspects have been covered in detail to equip students and teachers with standard analytical tools for approaching different challenging problems in Human-Economic Geography.

ACKNOWLEDGMENT

I delightedly extend my gratitude to all those whose viable contribution made me get encouraged and letter realizes a great success in the process of preparing this book. Specifically, I would like to extend my special thanks to my Heavenly God, and to all the authors of the textbooks and other literature that helped me to enrich this work, because their contribution in the production of this book is invaluable, reminiscent and hence unforgettable.

Likewise, I highly acknowledge my beloved mother; Coretha Karol, my most beloved wife; Mariam Lucas, my young brother; Majaliwa Philemon, my best and closely friends; Paul Enock Jangu, Samson Balele and others who supported the work of this book in order to be accomplished, especially my students and staff members in my teaching profession (at The University of Dodoma, Kiseke secondary school, Geita secondary school, Mirui secondary school, Kasololo secondary school, Wema academe and Liwale day secondary school). Special thanks should also go to Amazon Company for their great support as well as Naxfra Mixed Education Enrichment.

I wish to extend lots of thank to all those who might assist me but do not appear in this book, I appreciate their moral and any other form of assistance given in this book.

Mwl. Frank Philemon
+255762426746
naxfra@gmail.com
   © 2016

CONTENTS

PART ONE

ECONOMIC GEOGRAPHY

CHAPTER 01:

INTRODUCTION TO HUMAN ACTIVITIES

Human Activity defined as to what people do or cause to happen in order to achieve a certain goal in life. It is the act or process of producing certain things intended by people in a certain place, which can be a country, region, district or a village. It is also defined as the function or tasks or works curried out or done by human being over time for achieving certain purposes.

Forms of Human Activities
There are two types of human activities:

1. *Social human activities:* includes, human population and human settlement.

2. *Economic human activities*: Includes agriculture, tourism, energy and power, trade, transport and communication, mining, fishing among others.

Types of Human Activities:
(a) Five types of human Activities:
    1. Primary activities.
    2. Secondary activities.
    3. Tertiary activities.
    4. Quaternary activities.
    5. Quinary activities.

(b) Four types of human activities (i.e. quinary activities is the party of quaternary activities):
    1. Primary activities.
    2. Secondary activities.
    3. Tertiary activities.
    4. Quaternary activities.

General Types of Human Activities:
1. Primary human Activities: These are human activities that involve extracting raw materials directly from the Earth. Good example is; farming (agriculture), mining, fishing among others.

2. *Secondary human Activities:* These are human activities that involve processing and manufacturing of raw materials into useful products. For example; processing and making iron from ore, coffee pulping and sisal decortications, house making and construction to mention a few.

Note. Secondary activities they promote for the development of priming human activities.

3. *Tertiary human Activities:* These are the activities that involve the provision of services that are needed in the society. Example of services are; trade, tourism, education, hospital, transportation, Mechanics, banking, entertainment, advertising, legal seizes in courts, regions service (clerical services).

4. *Quaternary human Activities:* Are the activities that involve the provision of intellectual services in courts, religions and information. They include high tech industries with information technology, scientific research, library services, and computer based activities like making software.

In short, quaternary activities are considered to be new started in the last three decades.

5. *Quinary human Activities:* These are activities that done by executives or officials in fields under governments. They involve the highest level of decision making in society or economy.

Note: Quaternary and quinary are branches of the tertiary activities except that there are highly specialized activities that demand a lot intellectual inputs. Therefore, quaternary and quandary activities facilitate the primary and tertiary activities.

Economic Importance of Human Activities

The following below are some of the importance of human activities:

1. They facilitate development of manufacturing industries e.g. cultivation of cotton can lead to the development of textile industry.
2. Helps in creating employment in the country
3. Helps to abundant supply of food in the country e.g. agriculture, fishing and hunting

4. Activities like construction of roads contribute to the development of transport and communication network.
5. Recreational activities which turn and brings foreign currency.

Environmental Problems Caused by Human Activities

The environment al problems caused by human activities are as follow:

1. Pollution.
   a) *Air pollution.*
   b) *Water pollution.*
   c) *Soil/land pollution.*
   d) *Noise pollution.*
2. Deforestation.
3. Soil erosion.
4. Environmental degradation

Measures for Addressing Environmental Problems Caused by Human Activities

The following are some of the measures have to be undertaken so as to reduce or avoid or address the problems caused by human activities:

1. Proper use of methods of agriculture that involve environmental conservation.
2. Planting trees through afforestation and reafforestation where human activities are undertaken.
3. Provision of mass education that promote environmental protection.
4. Government should formulate policies and rules so as to rescue the environment.
5. Terracing the land, in order to reduce soil erosion that caused by water movements.
6. Destocking (reducing the number of livestock).

TRIAL QUESTIONS

1. Give the meaning of human activities.
2. With examples define the following terms:
   (1) Primary human activities.

    (2) Secondary human activities.

    (3) Tertiary human activities.

    (4) Quaternary human activities.

    (5) Quinary human activities.

3. Explain the importance of human activities.

4. Mention five human economic activities.

5. Mention four environmental problems that can be caused by human activities.

6. Suggest ways of solving or avoiding environmental problems that caused by human activities.

7. Name the human activities carried out around your school or home. How important is each of the human activities you have mentioned to your community?

CHAPTER 02:

AGRICULTURAL DEVELOPMENT

Crop cultivation called *arable farming* and an animal keeping called *pastoral farming* or *livestock husbandry*. Agriculture refers to the human activity that involves the cultivation of crops and keeping animals. Agriculture is also defined as the practice of cultivating land, growing crops as well rearing animals. Agriculture involves the following scope or coverage:

a) Small scale agriculture (subsistence agriculture)
b) Large scale agriculture (surplus agriculture)

A. SMALL SCALE AGRICULTURE

Small scale agriculture is the farming system that takes place on a small area (to produce food crops, cash crops and livestock keeping). This practiced for subsistence and not for commercial purpose. Small scale agriculture (Farming System) has the following characteristics:

1. Local superstition beliefs dominate among farmers.
2. There are poor farming methods involved.
3. Poor transport services.
4. The capital used is small (no intensive capital investment).
5. There are poor storage facilities.
6. Low or no uses of chemicals to control diseases and pests.
7. Farmers they use organic manure not industrial manure.
8. Farmers can grow perennial or annual crops.
9. The areas are small; usually the family labor is used.
10. Most of the crops are starchy and there is low production.
12. Simple tools are used, for example, the laud hoe and ox-drawn ploughs.
13. Varied poor methods of cultivation used, like shifting cultivation, intensive and sedentary subsistence farming.
14. Food crops such as maize, beans, millet, fruits and vegetables are the main types of crop grown.

Advantages of small-scale farming system (agriculture):

1. It is cheap because uses simple tools, with local manure and seeds.

2. It provides foods required to feed the population for example, maize, millet and wheat.
3. It has encouraged the development of settlement among the farmers.
4. It needs a small area of land, hence encourages the environmental conservation aspect.
5. It provides raw materials for the industries like cotton, tea and coffee.
6. Products like cotton, tea and coffee brings about foreign currencies. when are exported.
7. Farmers grow a variety of food crop and rear animals on a single plot.
8. The cost of labor is low because it mainly involves family members.
9. The different crops grown on a single plot make it easy to control pests since a single pest cannot attack all the crop varieties.
10. Since land mainly inherited, individuals acquire land at little or no cost.

Disadvantages of Small-scale Agriculture:

1. There is low production due to the use of simple tools and low diseases control.
2. Involves poor methods of agriculture that lead to environmental degradation like erosion and deforestation.
3. Poor quality of product due to use of poor farming methods and mechanization.
4. Low production encourages poverty among the farmers and their families.
5. Poor use of fertilizers can cause soil exhaustion.
6. Poor storage facilities, lead to losses of agricultural products.
7. This type of agriculture is highly dependent on favorable weather conditions. Bad weather condition results in great losses of crops.
8. Due to the small size of the farms it is not easy to invest effectively by using machines, instead of relying on manual labor.
9. The inter sire cultivations of the land makes the soil infertile after a while. This is especially so where farmers do not use manure or fertilizer.
10. Low crop yields and the small farm sizes results in small amounts of production.

Rapid Population Growth and Agriculture

Rapid population growth refers to fast increase in the number of people in an area. Rapid population grown has the following effects in small-scale agriculture:

1. It leads to the land degradation due to the clearing of vegetation and over cultivation.
2. There occurs shortage of food leading to the starvation or famine.
3. It leads to the pressure for land; hence, the needs of the people do not cope with the size of the available land. This leads to shortage of arable land.
4. Amount of rainfall decreases because of the clearing of vegetation for settlement and agricultural activities.
5. May cause for the shortage of food due to the high population leading to poor health condition among the farmers, hence agricultural activities may demise or decline.
6. Over cultivation of the land, the soil may lose soil fertility, as population increases, people need to produce more to cater their needs.
7. Due to rapid population growth, workers are cheap and easily available.
8. Small-scale farmers may change from subsistence farming to commercial farming to meet the needs of the growing population.

Ways of Improving the Subsistence Small-scale Agriculture:

1. The farmers should be educated in order that they can acquire new technology easily.
2. There should be control of population increase in order that, the number of people can match with the size and the potential of the land available.
3. Farmer should be encouraged to use modern farming techniques such as the use of machines and new varieties seeds.
4. There should be an improvement in infrastructure like roads and railways in an area.
5. Peasants should be given loan to invest in agriculture and introduce irrigation schemes where rainfall is unreliable.
6. Construction of better storage facilities and encouraging farmers to form cooperatives so that they can be able to organize agriculture smoothly and get assistance easily.
7. Communities and families should encourage their members to seek and buy land away their ancestral homes. This will help to reduce land fragmentation.
8. Since women are the main food producers in small-scale agriculture, they need to be empowered in family and community manners.

9. Measures should have to be taken to reduce the rate of population grown. This can be done through family planning education, discouraging polygamy and emphasizing the need to have small families that can be sustained on the available land resources.

Women Empowerment in Agriculture

Women empowerment can be defined as the process of giving women more power and equal right as men in all matter of political, social and economic decision making and participation. Also women empowerment is defined as the process of giving women more power and right to have control over the resources and more ability or liberty to participate in the agricultural activities. The following are the importance of empowering women in agriculture:

1. It promotes their abilities so that they can be able to participate more effectively in agriculture and other activities.
2. Gives women more confidence to be free in exposing out their own ideas pertaining to agriculture development.
3. It speeds up the development of agriculture by making women more efficient than before through making woman responsible in taking care on crops.
4. Women can become independent; lead their life by facing the problems confidently patterning agricultural matters.
5. It can enable women to create additional resources where resources were not enough in agricultural production.

Ways of Improving the Status of Women in Agriculture:
1. They have to be given enough opportunity for getting agricultural education in different level of education.
2. Women should be given right to own and inherit the land.
3. They should be encouraged to form some agricultural cooperation for easy assistance and loans provision
4. Women should be involved in decision-making process in the society, pertaining in agricultural activities.
5. Men also should be encouraged to cooperate with women in all agricultural activities.

Examples and Types of Subsistence Agricultural System

1. *Shifting Cultivation.*

In this, a peasant keeps on shifting from one place to another because of exhaustion of the land fertility in the system. This method of cultivation commonly practiced in tropical Africa, Central America and South East of Asia. The following are the features or characteristics of shifting cultivation:

(1) Simple tools are used in cultivation e.g. hand hoes, machetes.
(2) Sites or farms selected from virgin forests.
(3) It involves slashing and burning of grass and bushes.
(4) Most crops grown are starchy, such as maize, sorghum finger millet and bulrush millet.
(5) It takes place where there is low population and extensive area.
(6) The cultivation does not have permanent settlements.
(7) There is low production enough for food.

Advantages or Merits of Shifting Cultivation:
(1) The system is not costly since simple tools are used.
(2) A farmer assured of fertile soil due to the used of the virgin land.
(3) Food production assured because the family needs to obtain food rather than selling.
(4) Ashes obtained from burning bushes and forests add fertility or humus to the soil.
(5) No labor cost, only member of the family are involved.

Disadvantages or Demerits of Shifting Cultivation:
(1) There is low yield and hence no surplus of production.
(2) It is not for the farmers to sell the products, because it is hand to mouse agriculture.
(3) It cannot take place where there is high population.
(4) The use of fire kills microorganisms in the soil.
(5) There poor diets to the farmers since most of the crops grown are starchy in nature.
(6) It encourages deforestation due to felling of trees and poor method of cultivation.

2. Small Scale Sedentary Agriculture.

This farming system takes place when a farmer settled without moving from place to place. Examples of small-scale sedentary agriculture are *bush fallowing* and *intensive subsistence* farming. Small scale sedentary agriculture has the following advantages:

(1) It encourages the conservation of the land forest since farmers do not more from one place to another.
(2) A farmer can do several activation apart from agriculture due do the establishment of permanent are settlement.
(3) It facilitates the development of technology since the farmers are settled and car easily be assisted.
(4) It can take place where there is high population.
(5) The production is higher than in shifting cultivation.
(6) A farmer can get balanced diet and hence the health of the family members tends be good.
(7) There is technological advancement in agricultural activities.

Disadvantage of Sedentary Agriculture:

1. Sedentary Agriculture may lead to the loss of fertility of the land due to over cultivation on one area.
2. Too much use of modern fertilizers leads to land degradation.

3. Bush Fallowing

Bush fallowing refers to the system of agriculture whereby a farmer leaves idle the exhausted piece of land for a certain period of time in order to regain (replenish) its fertility. Merits of bush fallowing are:

(1) The system is not costly since the tools used are simple.
(2) Farmers do not waste of energy moving from one place to another, because farms are rotated.
(3) Fallowing allows regeneration of grass and bushes, which help in conserving the soil and replenishing its fertility.
(4) A piece of land that lies under fallow can be cultivated for a long time due to the use of rotation in the piece of lands available.
(5) Fallowing of the piece of land helps in controlling disease and pests.
(6) Production is higher than in shifting cultivation.

(7) Permanent settlement among farmers initially starts to development.

(8) Technological advancement starts to develop.

Demerits of Bush Fallowing:
   (1) The system requires that a farmer should have a large area for cultivation due to land rotation from year to year.
   (2) In high population the system cannot take place because of land rotation from year to year.
   (3) There is low yield because of the use of simple tools such as hoes and machetes during cultivation.
   (4) Inadequate use of chemical makes it difficult to control diseases especially when fallowing takes place for short time.
   (5) Since production is low, farmers fail to produce for commercial purpose; hence, they fail to generate capital.

B. LARGE-SCALE AGRICULTURE

Large-scale agriculture is the farming system, which takes place on a large area like sisal plantation, tea plantation, Rubber plantation and ranching. This type of agriculture carried out on large tracts of land for commercial purposes. Farmers aim at maximizing profit by selling crops.

Characteristics of large-scale agricultural system:
   (1) Production is high and in good quality of food.
   (2) It needs a lot of capital for investing.
   (3) The farmers are skilled.
   (4) It needs cheap and efficient transport system from the farms to the market and industrial Centre.
   (5) It is monoculture in nature.
   (6) High scale in the use of chemicals.
   (7) Some areas in the farm are irrigated instead of depending on rainfall only.
   (8) It takes place on a large area and the farms are large. Example plantation and ranches.
   (9) High technological advancement.

Forms of Large-scale Agriculture

Large-scale (large-scale arable) agriculture has the following two forms:
   (i) Plantation agriculture

(ii) Extensive mechanized grain cultivation

(I) Plantation Agriculture

It is a large-scale commercial farming in which cash crops are grown using mechanized methods. Plantation is also referred as *estate*. This system of agriculture if it is specialized on one grown crop is called *monoculture*. Example of plantation may be grown crops like coffee, sisal, tee, cocoa, cotton, sugar cane, palm oil, cloves, and pyrethrum. Characteristic of plantation of agriculture are:

1. It is monoculture by nature.
2. Commercial oriented.
3. Farms are owned by government, co-operatives, large companies or wealthy individuals.
4. Skilled labor hired to manage crop production while unskilled labor hired during planting, weeding and harvesting seasons.
5. Mechanization is common during activities, such as land preparation, planting, spraying and harvesting.
6. There is wide use of fertilizers to improve soil fertility and in turn increase production.

Requirements for Establishing Plantation Agriculture:
(1) There should be enough capital.
(2) Reliable supply of both skilled and unskilled labor.
(3) There should be ready market.
(4) There should be reliable transport system.
(5) There should be large area to allow this agricultural system.
(6) There should be efficient management.
(7) There should be reliable storage facilities and efficient processing unit
(8) There should be a conducive climate depending on the nature of crops to grown.

Advantages of Plantation Agriculture:
(1) The products are of high quality due to the use of advanced technology.
(2) There is surplus production due to the use of advanced technology and high decease control.
(3) There is high efficiency of the use of machinery.

(4) It creates employment to the people due to the high number of labors needed, hence reducing the problem of unemployment.

(5) It encourages the development of industries due to the huge amount of products supplied to the industries.

(6) Promotes development of transport system.

(7) It promotes the improvement of living standard of people.

Disadvantages of Plantation Agriculture:

1. It is monoculture in nature, hence encourages soil degradation.
2. In establishment of plantation agriculture large areas are cleared leading to desertification.
3. Most crops are for commercial purpose hence can lead to shortage of food.
4. It cannot be carried out where there is high population.
5. Local people are often exploited since they work much and are paid low wages.
6. It encourages labor migration leading to the decline in labor supply in other agricultural sectors like food crops production.
7. It easily suffers from price fluctuation in the world market.
8. It needs huge capital in its operation and establishment.

(II) Extensive Mechanized Grain Cultivation

Like plantation agriculture, this also involves the cultivation of crops on large tracts of land. Grains or cereals are the main crops grown in this type of large-scale agriculture; for examples; wheat, maize barley, rye and oats. Extensive mechanized grain cultivation has the following major crops as grown in large scale agriculture:

1. Coffee.

The coffee plant first identified in the south highlands of Ethiopia in the district of kaftans. The plant taken to Saudi Arabia where its beans were roasted and made into a drink. It then spread to the Middle East and later introduced to Europe by the Turks. The Dutch later introduced it to their colony of Indonesia. Missionaries introduced coffee in Tanzania from Reunion Island. Coffee is a beverage crop and is in different species. There three main types of coffees, namely:

 ℔ Arabica

♻ Robusta
♻ Liberia

Arabica: Arabica coffee is the most commercially important in the world trade. It originated from the mocha coffee indigenous to the Arabian Peninsula.

Robusta: Is the West African variety. It is hardy and yields poor quality coffee. It can survive in drier climate and is disease-resistance.

Liberia: Is also hardy and disease-resistant species. It is indigenous to Liberia and suited to lowland rather than to upland condition. It gives heavy yields of moderate-quality coffee.

Conditions for Growing Coffee:
1. Coffee requires rainfall of about 1500mm to 2550mm.
2. Constant high temperatures of around 32^0c (i.e. $14^0 - 26^0$ or $57^0f - 78^0f$)
3. It needs a lot of labor especially during the harvesting time.
4. Altitudes of between 900m to 2100m above sea level are suitable for coffee growing (highland are not suitable).
5. It can grow in different types of soil but the suitable soil should be acidic with pH of 5.3 to 6.0.
6. Shade is necessary to prevent direct sunlight from affecting the trees when they are still young.

Preparation of Farm for Coffee Cultivation:
* The field to be planted needs to be prepared at least six months in advance.
* Holes for the coffee plats are dug at least three months in advance and should be at least 0.6 x 0.6m and 0.6m deep.
* The rows are normally 1.7m apart and the spacing can be 3.0m x 2.4m (or 2.7m x 1.4m).

Ways in Which Coffee Can be Planted and Cared
Coffee is always propagated by seeds. Then seeds should be from high yielding trees or highbred seed from coffee research stations. The seeds are planted in a nursery which should be well sheltered from divest sunlight and should have light deep soil that is also well drained. Tree shades should be avoided.

The seedbeds watered every day for the first two weeks, after then to twice week germination takes 6 to 8 weeks. When seedling forms a pair of true leaves, they are transplanted into seedling beds. The seedlings are ready for transplanting in the fields when they are about 0.2 to 0.4m tall.

About 2 to 3 weeks before transplanting the seedling into the fields, the top soil from each hole in the field mixed with a tin full of cattle dung or compost manure and a little super phosphate fertilizer during the long rains season. Mulch should be added around the trees to protect the roots from sun or by sheltering with some shade from banana leaves or three branches.

Pruning is done according to the desired number of stems to be allowed to grow. If is single stem, the main stem is left to grow to a height of 69cm then it is cut at a height of about 53cm. It may be desired to keep two or more main stems. This is called multiple stem pruning. A single or two suckers is selected and left to grow up to 130cm after which it is cut at the height of 114cm. A final single sucker then selected, when it grows up to 183cm it is cut back to 168cm. Any additional suckers plucked off.

From the early stages, continuous, weeding is necessary to keep the field weed-free, improves water infiltration into the soil and gives better yields. Inter cropping with two crops like beans and even banana is desired at later stages to reduce soil erosion. Mulching can be used as a method of weed control and improving moisture retention by the soil. It is done after all weeds have cleared. Fertilizer like nitrogen, phosphate, potassium and magnesium are applied where soil fertility seems to exhaust. Where cattle and manure are available, they can also be used to improve the soil quality.

Harvesting Coffee
Harvesting coffee berries done by hand. Laborers hired to pick the coffee from the stalk for the high quality coffee; only the red-ripped berries are picked. This harvesting may start 3 to 4 years after planting. The harvesting interval is from 7 to 14 days. Some farmers dry the berries in the sun or collect to the centers then to be taken to the processing mills.

Coffee processing

The first step in processing is to separate the berries. At the mills, the outer skin removed from the berries pulping. Passing the berries through the machine to remove the cover the cover or pulping, then the beans are fermented. Fermentation can be done by heaping the beans for about 12 to 24 hours. Curing: Involves washing and sun drying. After curing the machines peel off two layers of inner husks. Then the beans winnowed and graded.

After grading, they are packed in sacks for export. The importing countries roast the beans and then grind them into powder, which is letter used to make beverage.

Note: Producing countries of coffee are Brazil, Uganda, Ethiopia, Angola, Senegal, Ivory Coast, Mexico, Indonesia, Guatemala, India, Kenya, Malagasy, Cameroon and Tanzania in Mbeya, Kilimanjaro, and Kagera.

Coffee can be Stored and Transported Through:
The coffee stored in warehouses awaiting its sale. These storage facilities must be well aerated to ensure the freshness of the beans. The bags of coffee are transported by road and railway to stores, factories and exporting ports.

2. Tea.
Tea is grown in many Tropical countries. It started in the valley in china during the 16th century. It first introduced in East Africa in the year of 1900 at Entebbe in Uganda. In 1903, it was introduced in Tanzania and Kenya. In Tanzania, tea grown in Mbeya, Arusha, Iringa, Tanga and Kagera which the most common variety planted is *Assam*.

Conditions for the tea growth:
1. The ideal temperature ranges for growing tea is between 15^0 and 30^0C and should not be below 21^0c during the growing period for eight months.

2. The mean annual rainfall should be between 1400mm and 1750mm.
3. Tea does well in plateaus and highland areas in the height of between 1500m and 2200m above the sea level.

4. The soil should be deep and well drained but able to retain water for the plants.

5. Soil pH should be slightly acidic with a pH of 4 to 6 with little calcium.

6. A lot of shade used to be an essential factor in the early days as it helps to increase yields.

7. Tea production is a labor-intensive activity, in field preparation, plating, weeding, pruning, picking and processing.

8. Good roads are required to transport the green leaves from the farms to factories in a required time.

9. Availability of capital is essential especially for the land preparation, planting and weeding.

Preparation of tea farms

Tea is mainly propagated from cuttings that are obtained from clones that have high yielding abilities and are of good quality. This is because seedlings take long in the nursery before they can be planted. The field is prepared when the cuttings are almost read for transplanting. Deep digging is important to turn the soil over. Hole should be at intervals of 0.7m or 0.9m and rows should be about 1.5m apart.

Planting and Caring Tea Crops:

1. The cuttings for transplanting should be in the height about 20cm long.
2. Transplanting done at the beginning of the rain season.
3. Fertilizers and manure may be added to the soil before planting.
4. Young tea plants may also be intercropped with other crops such as beans to act as Mulch and protect soil erosion.
5. Tea requires a lot of nitrogen before maturity hence nitrogenous fertilizers needed to the soil.
6. Pruning by cutting the tips of the main stem and the branches so as each branch to form more branches. The braces grow later ally to form a frame.

Forming frames for tea crops
Frames are formed in the following ways:
- a) Pegging
- b) Rings
- c) Formative pruning

Formative pruning it is done so as to discourage vertical growth. The main stem cut at height of about 15 to 40cm. Pegging and use of Rings is meant to encourage lateral way (side-ways) growth of branches.

Tea harvesting
At two years, the tea bushes are ready for harvesting. Harvesting involves plunking the two top leaves and a bud including their tender at the tip of each shoot. The plucked leaves are thrown in the basket, which each picker carries.

Tea processing
The tea leaves have to be taken to the factory quickly for processing because their quality deteriorates fast. At the factory, the first stage is to weigh the green leaves. They are then spread on large troughs and then left to wither for 20 to 24 hours. Moisture content has to be carefully controlled to ensure the leaves retain at least 50% of the original moisture. This process is called *withering* and it determines the sweetness of the product.

After withering, the leaves are passed through a set of rollers in a process known as *rolling*. The rollers break up the leaf cells and fibers. After rolling, the leaves are put in room with high temperature and humidity for about 3 to 4 hours; there they undergo *fermentation* or *souring*. After fermentation, the leaves dried by passing them through a drier at a temperature of about 104^{0}C, this process called *firing* or *roasting*. It meant to stop further fermentation. Moisture in the leaves is reduced to about 30%.

Storing and transporting tea
The processed tea is stored in large warehouses awaiting its sale. Tea is transported to factories and to customers by road, railway or by waterways.

Major world producers of tea

The leading tea producers of tea in the world are; India, China, Sri Lanka, Japan, former USSR, Kenya, Indonesia, Turkey, Bangladesh and Argentina.

3. Sugar Cane.

Sugar cane is a tropical reed-like plant with a thick stem that contains a sweet liquid. It belongs to the *saccharin* family. Sugar cane is a tropical crop whose origin believed to be East Asia. It spread to the Middle East then to southern Europe that introduced to the other parts of the world by the European explorers. In Tanzania, sugar cane is grown or cultivated in Arusha at Chini and in Morogoro at Kilombero among others.

Conditions for Growing of Sugar cane:
1. Sugarcane thrives best in hot climates with temperature ranging between 21^0C and 27^0C throughout the year.
2. It needs abundant rainfall of at least 1270mm, if it grows without irrigation.
3. Needs a well-drained soil.
4. The ideal topography for growing sugar cane is gently sloping land.
5. Infrastructure is required for transporting the sugar cane to the factories.
6. Sugar cane growing requires a lot of capital to pay workers and buy or use machinery such as Tractors and Lorries.
7. A lot of labors are needed.

Preparation of Farm for Sugar cane Growth
The fields to be planted is best prepared through ploughing by using tractors with wheels are used where the soil is manageable. On clay and black soil, crawler tractors are used because they do not stuck in the soil. When the land is ready, shallow furrows are made across the field. These are made in estimate 1.2m to 1.8m apart.

Planting and Caring Sugar cane
Sugar cane grown from cuttings of older sugar cane stems, which are between 8 and 14 months old. Each cutting has three nodes (called sets). The sets are laid in furrows horizontally, next to each other. In the growth of these sets forms a cluster of new shoots called *stool*. Weeding is done in 3 to 4 times before harvesting. Weeding also is done when the plants are still young and short. Some farmers they use herbicides to kill the weeds.

Harvesting Sugar cane
In East Africa the crop, take about 14 months to mature at coast while in the plateaus it may take up to 22 months. The cane harvested by cutting it at the base and removing the crown leaves. The cane has to be cut and delivered to the processing mills within 48 hours. The cut cane is collected by hand and loaded onto tractors or Lorries. On large plantation, loading may be done by mechanical means.

Sugar Cane Processing
At the factory, the cane first weighed while still on the Lorries or tractors. After it is offloaded it put in large tanks where it is washed. It then cut into pieces. The pieces are fed into rollers, which squeeze out the juice. The remanding fibers, known as *bagasse* is dried and used as fuel for the boilers. The juice is then put in boilers called *evaporators*. It boiled until it turns into thick syrup.

The syrup passed onto a vacuum pan under very low pressure to form a dark brown mixture of sucrose crystals and molasses called *massecuite*. This mixture is put in tanks called *crystallizers* where the sugar crystals grown. The resultant sugar in brown and has large crystals. The sugar undergoes further refining to produce brown and white sugars. The various grades of sugar are then packed in bags ready to be transported to the market.

How Sugar cane can be Stored and Transported?
The sugar is stored in bags of various sizes in large warehouse. It then transported to the market using Lorries, ships trains, or airplanes.

Major World Producers of Sugar cane
Leading producers of sugar cane are Brazil, India, Mexico, Pakistan, USA, Thailand, Australia, Colombia, South Africa and Indonesia. Other countries are Tanzania, Sudan, Uganda and Kenya.

4. Wheat
Wheat is a grass crop whose botanical name is *Triticum spp*. The grain is ground into flour, which is then used to make food such as breads and cakes.

Categories of Wheat

In a broad basis, wheat is classified into two groups based on the seasons of sowing:

(i) Winter wheat: is sown in late autumn or early winter and is ready for harvesting during early summer.

(ii) Spring wheat: is sown during spring and harvested in late summer or autumn.

Leading and Major Producers of Wheat

Leading and major producers of wheat are Russia, USA, China, India, Canada, France, Turkey, Australia, Pakistan, German, Romania, South Africa and Argentina. In East Africa Kenya is the leading producer followed by Tanzania.

Conditions for Growth of Wheat:

1. It requires a temperature of about 15^0C during the growing period and not exceeding 20^0C.
2. Require low rainfall that should be between 305mm and 1015mm.
3. The suitable soils are light clay or deep loam soil and should be well drained and provide proper anchorage to wheat stalk.
4. Rolling topography is good because it facilitates drainage and the use of machinery.
5. Large-scale wheat production requires extensive areas of sparsely populated land, which farms can occupy.

How Land or Farm for Wheat Growth can be Prepared?

Land is first cleared from bushes, twigs and grass. It then ploughed, during the dry season. By time of planting, most weeds would have germinated with the wheat would have been killed.

In Which Way Wheat can be Planted and Cared?

In large farms, sowing is done by using tractor driven seed drills. In addition, herbicides applied to control weeds while in small-scale, farmers pull out the weeds.

How wheat can be processed?

At the processing factory, the grains are cleaned several times to remove dirt such as stones, weed, seeds and any other kinds of unwanted items. Roller then crushes the grain. Where white wheat is desired, the grain covering separated from the inner part. The grain is then ground and sifted several times until the desired particle since are attained.

What can be the Real Storage and Transportation of Wheat?
The trucks and Lorries transport the grains to the stores for storage. After processing, the milled wheat is stored in warehouses in bags of various sizes, ready for transportation to the markets. Transportation is by use of Lorries, tractors, ships among others.

5. Maize
Botanic name of maize is *Zea Mays*. It has its origin among the *Incas* and *Aztecs* of South America. It is the staple food for many Latin America and African people. Explorers such as Columbus introduced it to Europe while Portuguese brought it to East African countries. Conditions for growth of maize are:

1. The crops thrive in the tropical as well as in the warm temperate climates.
2. Temperature of the day should be between 14^0C (night) to 30^0C (day).
3. Annual rainfall needed for maize to grow is between 635mm to 1145mm and in Africa, annual rainfall between 300 to 1800mm.
4. The soil should be deep and rich in nutrients. The soil also should be well drained.
5. Altitude should be 2900m above sea level.
6. Availability of labors is very important.
7. Sufficient capital is highly needed for high scale plantations of maize.
8. Sufficient storage of grain production is required.
9. Market and transportation availability is needed.

How the Farm or Land for Growing Maize can be Prepared?
Tractor drawn plough is commonly used on large-scale farms to prepare the land. A field may be ploughed three times and harrowed up to five times to produce a fine soil. In small-scale farms, land preparation done by digging by using hoes and ox-drawn ploughs may be used.

How maize can be Planted and cared?

This is done at the beginning of the rainy season, unless it is grown under Irrigation. Planting it is done when the soil is dry or slightly wet. The space between hole and rows is determined by the type of maize variety and the prevailing climate. The space between holes may vary between 23cm and 30cm while the rows may be between 0.6m and 0.9m apart.

Fertilizers are widely used because they increase yields. Regular weeding is done during the growing period until the crop reaches a height of 405cm. In drier areas, it is desirable to continue weeding until the plants start flowering. This is due to reduction of competition for moisture in the soil. Pesticides and insecticides used if possible.

How maize can be harvested?

Maize is left to dry in the field while it still on its stalk. On large farms, the stalks are cut and pilled in the field in pyramidal peaks called stocks. The maize cobs are later removed by hand after being dry.

How maize can be processed?

Removing the seeds from the cob (shelling) is done by use of machines. Shelling is done by hand on small-scale farms. The grain is then winnowed to remove any impurities and poorly formed grains.

How Maize can be Stored and Transported?

The grain may be put in sacks for transportation to collecting or buying centers. Extensive farmers store their grain in grain silos. Depending on where the market is, the grain is transported using various means.

Major world Producers of Maize

The leading country produces of maize (commercially) are USA, France, China, Argentina, Brazil, India, Italy, Romania, Hungary, Yugoslavia and South Africa.

Category of Crops, and Leading Producers of Such Category of Crop:

Category	Crop	Leading Producing Countries
1. Cereals	(a) Rice	China, India, Indonesia, Japan, Bangladesh

	(b) Wheat	Russia, China, USA, India, Canada.
	(c) Maize	USA, China, Brazil, Russia, Romania, South Africa.
	Barley	Russia, China, Canada, UK, France.
	Oats	Russia, USA, Canada, Germany Poland.
2. Beverages	(a)Tea	India, China, Sri Lanka, Japan, Kenya.
	(b) Coffee	Brazil, Colombia, Cote d'Ivoire Mexico Uganda.
	(c) Cocoa	Ghana, Cote d'Ivoire, Brazil, Nigeria, Cameroon.
	(d) Sugar cane	India, Brazil, Cuba, China, Mexico.
3. Fibres	(a) Cotton	USA, Russia, China, India, Brazil.
	(b) Flax	Russia, Poland, France, Romania, Egypt
	(c) Jute	China, India, Bangladesh, Thailand, Brazil.
	(d) Sisal	Brazil, Tanzania, Kenya, Angola, Madagascar.
4. Animal Fibres	(a) Wool (sheep)	Australia, Russia, New Zealand, Argentina, South Africa
	(b) Silk	Japan, China, South, Korea Russia, India.
5.Industrial Crops	(a) Rubber	Malaysia, Thailand, Indonesia, India, Sri Lanka.
	(b) Palm oil	Malaysia, Nigeria, Indonesia, India Cote d'Ivoire
	(c) Coconuts	Philippines, Indonesia, India, Sri Lanka, Malaysia.
	(d) Soya beans	USA, China, Brazil, Argentina.
	(e) Tobacco	China, USA, India, Brazil, Russia
6. Fruits	(a) Apples	USA, France, Italy, Germany, Poland.
	(b) Citrus fruits	USA, Brazil, Japan, Italy, Spain.
	(c) Date	Egypt, Iraq, Iran, Indonesia, Ecuador, Thailand.

General Advantages (Importance) Of (Growing) Cash Crops in a Country:

(1) They encourage development of industries, for example the cultivation of cotton lead to the development textile industries.
(2) They contribute to generation of capital and the government revenue.
(3) They stimulate the development of transport and communication systems.
(4) They lead to the creation of employment opportunities.
(5) Encourage the improvement of the living standard of people in a country.

Agricultural Activities in Tanzania

Agriculture in Tanzania is the sector that employs about 80% of Tanzanians. Nevertheless, the majority of Tanzanians they engage in small-scale agriculture and minority in large-scale agriculture. Apart from providing employment, agriculture in Tanzania provides food and raw materials that needed in industries. The following is the table that shows crops production in Tanzania:

Crops	Areas of Production
1. Cashew nuts	Mtwara, Ruvuma, (Tunduru), Lindi, Coast region, Dar es salaam and Tanga
2. Tobacco	Tabora, Ruvuma, Iringa, Mbeya, Rukwa, (Mpanda), and Kagera (Biharamro and Ngara).
3. Cotton	Mwanza, Shinyanga, Tabora, Mbeya (Chunya and Mbozi), Morogoro.
4. Sugar cane	Morogoro, Mwanza, Rukwa, Arusha, Kagera.
5. Tea	Iringa, Mbeya, Kilimanjaro and Tanga (Usambara).
6. Cloves	Zanzibar and Pemba
7. Pyrethrum	Iringa, Mbeya, Arusha, Manyara (Mbulu and Hanangi), Moshi.
8. Sisal	Morogoro, Coast region, Lindi, Mtwara, Tanga.
9. Groundnuts	Dodoma, Rukwa, Mbeya, Iringa, Singida, Tabora, Shinyanga, Kigoma, Tanga, Mtwara and Ruvuam.
10. Coconuts	Mtwara, Lindi, Mafia, Zanzibar, Pemba, Dar es salaam, Coast region, Tanga and Morogoro.
11. Wheat	Arusha, Manyara, Kilimanjaro, Mbeya, Iringa, (Ludewa) and Ruvuma (Songea).

Challenges or Limitations Facing Cash Crop Production in Tanzania

The following are some of the problems facing cash crop production in Tanzania:

1. Diseases and pests that attacks the crops both in the farms and in or at the storage facilities.
2. Price fluctuation in the market, which tends to discourage farmers.
3. Poor transport and communication systems.
4. Poor climate conditions like unreliable rainfall, which sometimes can be too much or sometimes too little.
5. Decline of soil fertility due to over cultivation of the farms and leaching.
6. Frequent fires that end up devastating (destroying) the crops in the farms.
7. Conflicts between farmers and pastoralists like at Kilosa in Morogoro region
8. Low level of technology associated with the used of simple tools.
9. Rapid population growth, which has forced people to concentrates on food crop production rather than on cash crop production.

Limitations (Drawbacks) of Large-scale Farming in Tanzania:

1. Low capital for investment.
2. Land is becoming smaller and smaller due to the increase in population and land degradation.
3. There are frequent tribal conflicts like those in Mara and Morogoro between pastoralists and agriculturalists.
4. There is poor support from the government.
5. Climatic problems like drought and too much rainfall that causes floods.
6. Price fluctuations and especially low prices that discourage the farmers.
7. Rural-urban migration leads to the problems of labor supply.
8. Mismanagement of funds set for agriculture.
9. Poor agricultural policies.

Causes of Land Conflicts in Africa

Below are some of the major causes of land conflict in Africa:

1. Population pressure that has led to the shortage of land in some areas.
2. Poor Agricultural policy which does not state properly on how to undertake agricultural activities.
3. Lack of land tenure, such that farmers are not given special land to own.
4. Poverty that makes people keeps on depending on the land rather than investing in other sectors of economy.
5. Customs and traditions by which farmers keep on claiming the ownership of land left by their ancestors who were the clan members.
6. Some tribes like portraying their superiority over other tribes
7. Environmental problems like soil degradation and lack of land for pasture have made farmers to be in conflict when migrating to new area in search of better land for cultivation or pasture.
8. Colonial legacy in which the foreigners were favored more than the indigenous people to own land in the country.

Measures to be taken so as to alleviate the Problem of Land Conflicts
The following measures should be taken so as to avoid the problems of land conflict in any country of Africa:

1. Other activities apart from agriculture should be created so as to reduce conflict on land.
2. The farmers should be encouraged to control population increase.
3. Government should formulate good policies that govern agricultural activities and land ownership.
4. Capital should be given to the farmers so as they can be able to invest in better agricultural methods in order to make production very high in a small area or small number of animals.
5. Farmers should be encouraged to settle in one place to avoid clashes and conflicts.

Contributions of Cash Crop Farming to the Economy of USA and Tanzania

The United States of America (USA) unlike Tanzania is an industrialized country. It is among the world's leading economic powers. As such, its agriculture is very advanced. Tanzania is the second to Brazil in sisal production worldwide. The following are some of the contributions of cash crop faming in both Tanzania and USA:

1. Cash crops provide raw materials to the industries hence lead to the development of industries.
2. Cash crops farming are the source of income to many farmers is USA and Tanzania.
3. Cash crop act as the source of foreign exchange in USA and Tanzania.
4. Reduces or eliminate the burden of importation at cash crop from other countries on the two countries. This is because there are abundant cash crops in these countries.
5. Production of cash crops has led to the improvement of transport and communication in the areas where cash crops are grown.
6. Cash crops production has led to the provision of employment opportunity to the people.

Problems Facing Large Scale Agriculture in USA and Tanzania:

1. *Climatic hazards.* Large scale agriculture is affected by several climatic hazards like extreme strong winds.

2. *Pests and diseases.* On large farms, an outbreak of pests and diseases destroys large area of crops.

3. *Poor management.* Mismanagement like embezzlement of funds provided to support the large farms is a big problem. This problem slows the development of large scale farming.

4. *Deterioration of soil fertility.* Loss of soil fertility caused by leaching due to high rainfall, monoculture, and frequent use of machinery. This is the problem because soil infertility reduces the productivity of crops.

5. *Market flooding.* This is due to the large amounts of products supplied to the people than what they want, hence low prices for agricultural products.

6. *Expensive inputs*. Large scale agriculture needs a lot of inputs hence farmers may not afford to buy them because they are many and are in high price.

7. *Land encroachment*. Large scale agriculture is practiced on very large pieces of land hence those who don't have land may invade these farms thus leading to conflict.

Ways of Improving Large Scale Agriculture in Tanzania

The following are outlines of how Tanzania can solve these problems and therefore improve its large-scale agriculture:

1. *Expansion and improvement of agricultural storage facilities*. This may reduce the losses of crop due to the spoilage. In addition, this may facilitate the farmers to store their products safely and for long period.

2. *Management improvement*. The managers of large-scale farms should be trained and educated about proper financial managements so as to reduce chances of embezzlement and other forms of frauds.

3. *Protection of pests and diseases*. This should be done through using clear monitoring and research on crops so as to detect the presence and treatment for the presence of any pests and disease that attacking the crops.

4. *To improve soil fertility*. To improve soil fertility, fertilizers and manure should be used, so as to increase production. In addition, this can be improved through the application of mulching, and intercropping so as to reduce leaching.

5. *Provision of subsidies*. Subsidies; refers to the government meeting part of the cost of something. Through the government, providing and offering subsidies on inputs such as fertilizers and seeds may encourage farmers to cultivate more crops, so as to expand large scale-agriculture in the country.

6. *Proper application of land encroachment.* This can be alleviated through proper fencing of property offering jobs to those people living near the farms, or digging boreholes and building classroom among others.

Livestock Keeping or Livestock Farming

Livestock refers to animals and birds kept or raised in a farm. Again, livestock keeping or pastoral farming or livestock farming it is referred to the rearing of animals and birds. Livestock farming can be distinguished into *Traditional (subsistence) livestock farming* and *modern (commercial) livestock farming*. Therefore, there are three major forms of livestock keeping:

1. Pastoralism.
2. Sedentary livestock keeping.
3. Commercial livestock keeping.

Pastoralism

Pastoralism is the practice of rearing pasture-dependent animals such as cattle, goats, camels and sheep. *Nomadism* is the most common form of pastoralist in some region transhumance practiced. This is the seasonal movement of herdsmen in between low land and highland in search of water and pasture.

Sukuma, and Nyamwezi of Tanzania are some of the tribes that practice transhumance. There are reasons behind for the decline of pastoralism now days: *Lack of land for pasture, Political boundaries and control. Education that given to the people about other better methods of animal keeping* and *Government policy that discouraging the method of keeping animals.*

I. Traditional (Subsistence) Livestock Keeping

Traditional livestock keeping have the following forms:

a) Nomadic pastoralism.
b) Semi-nomadic or semi sedentary pastoralism.
c) Sedentary livestock keeping.

(A) *Nomadic Pastoralism*

Nomadic pastoralism is defined as livestock farming in which pastoralists constantly move from place to place in search of pasture and water. Nomadic pastoralism is also called *nomadic herding*.

A parson who moves from one place to another in search of pasture and water is a *nomad*. Examples of tribes that practice this system of livestock keeping are; Fulani in Nigeria, Maasai in Tanzania and Kenya, Nubi in South Africa among others.

Characteristics of nomadic pastoralism:
1. Cattle kept for prestige, paying bride price and not for sale.
2. The breading process is uncontrolled.
3. The herds of animals are large in size.
4. The land is communally owned.
5. The diseases are common because of poor care given to animals e.g. Farmers do not vaccinate their animals.
6. Low technology is involved.
7. Animals are of poor quality (poor health) and of low value.
8. The method is not expensive.
9. There is no permanent settlement as farmers move constantly with their animals.
10. The is a no crop cultivation and here animals are the sole base or support of the family life.
11. Many animals are grazed on the same area.
12. The system takes place where there is sparse population.

Advantages of nomadic pastoralism:
1. The system is cheap; it does not need advanced technology or sophisticated tools.
2. It assures the family the availability of food especially when the animals are so many.
3. The traditional varieties of animals are resistant to diseases and other environmental hardships.

Disadvantages of nomadic pastoralism:
1. Animals give poor production and are of low value.

2. Many animals die due to lack of disease and pests control.
3. A farmer waster a lot of time moving from place to place.
4. Cause desertification and soil erosion due to overgrazing and movement of many animals from one place to another.
5. It cannot take place where there is high population.

(B) Semi-Nomadic (Semi-Sedentary) Pastoralism
Semi-nomadic pastoralism is the system whereby animal keepers start settling and growing crops apart from keeping animals. Examples of tribes practicing this are Sukuma (Tanzania) and Karamanjong (Uganda).

(C) Sedentary Livestock Farming
It is the system by which farmers keep animal while settled permanently in one place.

Factors that made to the shift from nomadic to sedentary pastoralism:
1. The advancement in technology and the increase in the level of education among the people.
2. The increase in the size of population has led to the decrease in the size of the pastureland in which discourages nomadic system.
3. Government policies that encourage animal keepers to settle rather than moving from places to place.
4. The reactions by the environmentalists, which encourage environmental conservation by avoiding shifting animal keeping.
5. Pastoralists themselves have engaged in other activities like crop production, fishing hence permanent settlement established to them.

Characteristics of sedentary livestock farming:
1. The method uses more advanced technology than in nomadic technology.
2. The number of animals is not so high, that can be managed easily.
3. The animals kept in sheds; some can be fed using fodder as zero grazing.
4. There is high possibility of animal diseases control.
5. The system can take place where there is high population.

Note: Zero grazing is the situation in which animals given feeds in their shed without making them to go into the field to obtain pastures.

Advantages of sedentary livestock keeping:
1. The animals are healthy and hence breeding is high.
2. Since a limited number of animals kept, there is better care of animals in terms of disease control and food supply.
3. Pastoralists do not waste time moving from place to place.
4. It encourages the improvement of environment and its resources (environmental conservation)
5. It enable pastoralists to engage in other activities like agriculture
6. Manure can be used in the gardens and other crops in the farms.
7. Farmers get balanced diet since there is availability of both proteins and carbohydrates.
8. Pest and disease control is frequently done.
9. This type of livestock keeping is carried out in a small size of land.
10. It is suitable to the populated areas.

II. Commercial Livestock Keeping

Commercial livestock keeping refers to the rearing of livestock for meat, milk or wool, which is then sold to earn income. Alternatively, it is the system of keeping animals and birds for commercial purpose, for example ranches and dairy farming. *Ranch* is the rearing of livestock on an extensive piece of land while *Dairy farming* is the rearing of livestock for the production of milk.

Benefits of Livestock Farming in any country
1. Livestock are source of food, like milk and meat.
2. The hides and skins of some animals are used traditionally as clothing and for making leather to make bags, shoes and belts.
3. Act as source of income to the farmers from sold animals, meet and other animal's products.
4. Livestock keeping and industries that process livestock products provide employment opportunities.
5. Livestock keeping encourages development of industries that process animal products.

6. Livestock keeping is the source of revenue through taxes collected to the animal owners.

Problems Facing Livestock Keeping in any country:
1. Insufficient capital to buy inputs like pesticides and pay for animals, medicine, medical services and tax.
2. Poor efficient due to the use of little or no technology.
3. Change of climate that may lead to the shortage of water and pastures.
4. Attacked by pests and disease that lead to loss of livestock.
5. Absent of clear market or drop in demand for livestock products.
6. Lack of proper and adequate training on livestock keeping leads to low production and losses.

Solutions to the Problems Facing Livestock Keeping:
1. The government has to subsidize inputs such as pesticides to make them affordable.
2. Farmers should be encouraged to adopt modern technology of livestock keeping so as improve their production.
3. Eradication of disease that attacks animals through treating and vaccinating livestock.
4. Various breeds that are suitable for various climatic conditions should be developed.
5. Proper care and feeding should be considered in order to increase the value and quality of livestock and their products.
6. Transport and infrastructure should also be improved in order to increase the supply of livestock and their products in the market
7. Farmers should be educated and trained on the best livestock keeping methods.

Animal Husbandry in Tanzania

Livestock production is one of the major agricultural activities in Tanzania. The sector contributes to national food supply and GDP. Action taken by the government to ensure that livestock keepers obtain formals legal recognition of traditional grazing rights as envisaged in the new land act.

Forms of Livestock Keeping in Tanzania

The following are outlines of the forms of livestock keeping in Tanzania:

1. Pastoralism: This type of livestock keeping is practiced by communities living in areas that have a lot of land for pasture, for example the Maasai, Sukuma, Nyamwezi among others. Most of these communities in the country practice semi-nomadic where they have permanent homes but move their livestock to greener pastures when their home areas are dry. Cattle are the main type of livestock kept.

2. Sedentary livestock keeping: Communities that live in areas with a high population like in urban and semi-urban areas of Tanzania practice sedentary livestock keeping. Dairy cattle are the main type of livestock kept. Cattle kept in zero grazing while other animals are kept in their shelters.

3. Commercial livestock keeping: This practiced where extensive land is easily available. It is carried out in both the highlands and dry areas of the county. Cattle, sheep and goats are the main types of livestock kept. In this, animals often given food supplements, especially those kept for dairy purposes. In ranches, many animals are kept and there is little or no food supplements given to the livestock.

4. Subsistence livestock keeping: This refers the keeping of livestock for consumption by the farmers and his or her family. It is practiced by all communities in Tanzania. The main livestock kept are cattle, goals and chicken. The farmers do not feed the animals any food supplement except salt for cattle, goats and sheep.

Economic Importance of Livestock in Tanzania

The following are reasons of livestock keeping being important economically in Tanzania:

1. Source of food.
2. Important for industrial development.
3. Source employment opportunity.
4. Source of government revenue.

5. Promote for trade development.
6. Facilitate for development and improvement of transport.

Comparison and Contrast of Livestock Keeping in Australia and Tanzania
Livestock keeping in Tanzania and Australia has some similarities and differences as follow:

Similarities:
1. In both countries, there are common types of livestock kept; that is cattle, goats, sheep and poultry.
2. Animals and animals' products sold in both countries. Some of the common products include meat and milk.
3. Livestock keeping in both countries practiced at both of subsistence and commercial level.
4. Sedentary livestock keeping practiced in both countries; this done in areas that are highly populated.
5. Dairy farming in both countries carried out in areas that have adequate rainfall and plenty of grass.
6. Ranching in Tanzania and Australia carried out in the sparsely populated areas. In Tanzania, National Ranching Company (NARCO) owns this.

Differences:
1. In Australia more scientific methods are employed in the management and running of livestock keeping compared to Tanzania.
2. Livestock keeping in Australia is more advanced than in Tanzania especially in the use of machinery like in milking and sheep shearing.
3. The breads of livestock reared in Australia yield more than those kept in Tanzania.
4. Livestock kept in Tanzania geared more towards meeting local demand. In Australia, it is geared towards the export market.
5. In Tanzania, the main types of livestock kept are cattle while in Australia the main type of livestock kept are sheep.

6. Pastoralism and sedentary livestock keeping are the main type of livestock keeping practiced in Tanzania while in Australia, ranching is the main type of livestock keeping.

TRIAL QUESTIONS

1. Define the following terms:

a) Subsistence agriculture.
b) Commercial agriculture.
c) Transhumance.
d) Shifting cultivation.
e) Arable farming.
f) Horticulture.
g) Extensive farming.
h) Pastoral farming.
i) Multi cropping (poly culture).
j) Bush fallowing.
k) Floriculture.
l) Intensive farming.
m) Fallowing.
n) Agriculture.
o) Monoculture.
p) Mixed farming.
q) Zero grazing.

2. Outline the main characteristics of small-scale agriculture at a subsistence level.

3. What are the advantages of small-scale agriculture in Tanzania?

4. Identify the disadvantages of small-scale agriculture at a subsistence level.

5. Show how subsistence small-scale agriculture can be improved in Tanzania.

6. Identify the effects of rapid population growth on people's life quality.
7. Describe how population pressure can affects the subsistence small-scale agriculture.

8. Identify the ways through which women contribute in small-scale agriculture in Africa.

9. What problems are women facing in their participation in small-scale agriculture?

10. Show the characteristics of:
   a) Shifting cultivation.
   b) Sedentary subsistence farming.

11. Identify and explain the advantage and disadvantages of the following:
   a) Shifting cultivation.
   b) Sedentary agriculture.
   c) Bush fallowing.

12. Outline the problems facing small-scale agriculture in your country.

13. Explain the way of improving small-scale agriculture in Tanzania.

14. State the difference between subsistence small-scale agriculture and commercial large-scale agriculture.

15. Outline the factors hindering the development of large-scale agriculture in Tanzania.

16. What are the problems caused by large farming in any country?

17. (a) What are the advantages and disadvantages of plantation agriculture?
   (b) What are the major requirements for the development of plantations in any Country?

18. Show main six characteristics of plantation agriculture.

19. List six crops that are involved in the plantation agriculture and mention areas where they are grown.

20. Mention the areas where wheat, cotton, sisal, ground runts, coconuts, tea, and sugarcane are grown in Tanzania.

21. Define and write short notes on the following terms;
   a) Ranch.
   b) Ranching.
   c) Mulching.
   d) Beef farming (beef production).
   e) Dairy farming.
   f) Destalking.

22. Mention the ranches that found in Tanzania.

23. What are the factors hindering the development of ranches in Tanzania?

24. Identity the advantages and disadvantages of ranching in Tanzania.

25. Outline the factors that have led to the development of beef farming in USA.

26. Shows the role of sheep farming to the economy of South Africa.

27. Identify the measure can be used in combating the problems facing large-scale farming in East Africa.

28. How does the rapid population grown affects livestock farming in Africa?

29. Show the effects of livestock farming on the environments.

30. Why is mixed farming more developed in the USA Corn Belt than in Tanzania?

31. Name and explain in short two plantation crops and two cereal crops grown on large scale agriculture in Tanzania.

32. (a) Describe five conditions that favor tea growing
      (b) Describe how tea is processed in the factory

(c) Name three major producer of tea in the word.

33. (a) Describe the main characteristics of pastoralism.

(b) Explain how livestock keeping in Australia differ from that in Tanzania.

34. (a) The activities known as agriculture is now days including _____, _____ and _____.

(b) What do you understand by the term "zero grazing"?

CHAPTER 03:

WATER MANAGEMENT FOR ECONOMIC DEVELOPMENT

Water is a clear liquid, without colour or taste, which falls from the sky as rain and is necessary for animal and plant life. Water management refers to the skillful or wise use of water resources. The following are the uses of water:

1. Domestically water is used for cooking, washing, sanitation and drinking.
2. It used in industries for cooling engines and processing.
3. Used in Construction activities.
4. Used in recreational purpose like Swimming.
5. Used as medicine for curing skin diseases because they contain different minerals and chemicals.
6. Water used as source of power or energy especially of hydroelectric power (HEP).
7. Water is important for supporting lives of plants and animals.
8. Water bodies act as source of rainfall through evaporation.
9. Water is used in farms to support agriculture that is, in the irrigation schemes and other farms that need natural water from rainfall.

Economic Importance of Water:

1. It encourages industrial development since water is used in cooling machine, processing and purifications.
2. Water has led to the development of fishing industries.
3. Water encourages development of tourism through presence of different water bodies like rivers, oceans and seas, lakes, dams, beaches
4. It supports development of agricultural sector through presence of water for irrigation and water from rainfall.
5. Water improves the family life since it is used for cooking, drinking, washing.
6. Selling water in cities and in towns is used as the source of capital to individuals.
7. Water act as the source of power for different economic development and uses.
8. It stimulates the development of transport and communication.
9. Water encourages soil formation.

Sources of Water

There are three main sources of water, as namely below:
- a) *Surface water sources*: These include lakes, melting snow cover, and dams.
- b) *Under ground water sources*: these involve springs and wells.
- c) *The atmosphere sources (meteoric water):* This involves precipitation in forms of rainfall, snowfall and hail coming directly from the atmosphere.

Problem Associated With Water:

(1) It tends to become scarce in many place of the world.
(2) Water pollution is common in many water sources.
(3) The sources are located very far from the home stead.
(4) Water supply services are expensive especially in towns.

Water Supply

Water supply refers to the provision or distribution of water making water available to the society for different purposes

Factors Affecting Water Supply

There is a very close relationship between quality of life and water. An adequate and reliable water supply improves the quality of life of people. The following are the factors affecting water supply:

(1) Climate: If an area has low rainfall the supply is limited or tend to be poor, while where there is high rainfall the supply of water is reliable.

(2) Gender Socio – Cultural Discriminatory Practice: In most societies, it is women who are involved in the supply of water in the families; hence, supply tends to be poor due to lack of cooperation of men in the water supply.

(3) Economic Level: Water in the societies is economically advanced the water supply system are well development and effective. While in poor societies water supply tends to be poor due to the financial problems, especially in rural areas.

(4) Water pollution due to oil spills, poisoning, dumping of wastes leads to problems in water supply: People avoid the sources, which have been polluted because they can get problem of diseases like cholera, typhoid, dysentery and diarrhea

(5) Water Uses: The uses of water are so varied such that the available water supply is under high competition, because water is needed for irrigation, for industrial activities, mining, tourism and agriculture.

(6) Poor Supply and Storage Facilities: Most of the supply and storage facilities are very old and others are no longer functioning. This leads to the water supply problems unlike to the place where facilities are good.

(7) Governments: Governments can facilitate good water supply if they formulate good policies encouraging the supply of good and adequate water.

(8) The Level of Education among the People: If people are well educated they can facilitate better supply of water by using it wisely and properly but if people are not educated ones the use of available resource unwisely.

(9) The Distance to the Water Sources: If water resources are near the homestead then the supply can be effective unlike if the sources of water are very far from the residential areas as well as to the economic sector.

(10)   Vegetation: Vegetation has both negative and positive influence on water supply. Negatively, some vegetation absorbs a lot of water leading to the shortage of water supply. Positively, vegetation can encourage water supply by forcing water into the ground storage, preventing excessive evaporation, contributing to the rainfall formation and preventing pollution by checking surface run off.

(11)   The Size of The Family: Domestic water supply tends to be poor or inadequate where the family members are so many hence people get problems in drinking, washing and cooking. Poor domestic water supply can cause outbreak of diseases and unsanitary condition, which affect the

life of the people. In most communities in Tanzania, girl child is affected than boy child in term of water supply from the distant water sources. The distance affects the girl child as follows:

    a) Girls wastes a lot of time looking for water. This brings to them tiredness or fatigue hence may not study effectively.
    b) Girls cannot effectively participate in other important aspects of the society like studying sport and games.
    c) In addition, the girl child is exposed to many accidents like being attacked by lions, bitten by snakes and sexual harassment.

How the Long Distance to Water Sources Affects the Girl Child?
(A) The distance between the home and the water sources affects the girl child in the following ways:
    (i)   If the distance is long, girls have to walk long distances to fetch the water, hence consume a lot of time.
    (ii)   May be attacked or molested along the way.
    (iii)   They lack time for studying and playing.
    (iv)   They become tired, hence no much attention to pay in the classroom hence poor performance.
    (v)   This may lead to illiteracy because girl child fell to go to schools, hence early marriage and birth.

(B) If the distance from the home, to water sources is short, then girls:
    (1) Would spend less time in fetching water.
    (2) They may have more time to play and go to school.
    (3) They can be able to pay attention to the class and do well academically.

Effects of Water Shortage in the Society:
1. Causes industrial decline because water needed for cooling and cleaning are not enough.
2. Decline in agriculture since crops cannot grow well.
3. Outbreak of diseases like cholera due to poor sanitary conditions caused by the shortage of water.
4. The family members especially women travel very far in search of water, hence fatigue and health deterioration.
5. Decline in fishing industries.

6. Death of plants leading to the desertification and soil erosion as well
7. Occurrences of drought.
8. Conflicts may occur among people in the society due to the shortage of water.
9. May cause for migration of people from the place lacking source of water to another place that have enough water.

Water Conservation

Water conservation refers to the process of preserving water for proper or suitable uses. An important question someone should ask himself or herself is that, *why should water be conserved?* The answer would be, water should be conserved due to the following reasons:

1. To ensure constant supply of water.
2. To satisfy the increased needs of water to the population.
3. To lower the costs of living since water charges set by the water supply units are high.
4. To avoid time wastage to the girl children and women so as to be able to do other economic activities and schooling.
5. To facilitate environmental conservations by introducing irrigation schemes as well as to ensure a reliable supply of hydroelectric power.
6. To improve the health conditions of family members especially women and girls who are largely affected through and fetching water.

Ways of Conserving Water Sources:

1. Building dams and barrages across rivers.
2. Through afforestation and reforestation programs.
3. Declaring some of the areas as protected areas by laws so that trees cannot be destroyed by people through cutting for different purposes.
4. Preventing water pollution through educating people to stop dumping waste product in the water bodies and avoiding the disposing of sewage materials (effluent) in the rivers, lakes and recycling of the wastes from different places.

Water Supply and Sanitation Improvement:

1. Permanent wells should be constructed near the homesteads.
2. Protecting springs by fencing to keep away from animals.

3. Controlling the population growth through family planning and the control of migration.
4. There should be proper use of water especially in the well-organization economic sectors.
5. Providing pipes and drains to keeps the areas clean.
6. Latrines should be well designed to improve sanitation.
7. Trees should be planted so as to reduce excessive evaporation and water pollution.
8. There should be cooperation between women and men on the water supply and conservation of water sources.

Advantages of Clean Safe Water and Sanitation:

1. People may become healthier.
2. Women who carry water from the sources may have shorter distance to walk.
3. People can have chances to engage themselves in other economic activities effectively.
4. People may improve their life standards.
5. Girl children can have ample time to concentrate on studies instead of thinking where to get water for their family uses.

Hydroelectric Power (H.E.P)

Hydroelectric power is the power generated under the influence of waterfall. The following are the conditions for harvesting or harnessing (tapping water for) hydroelectric power:

1. Reliable rainfall over high mountains in order to ensure the supply of water and presence of big sources of water.
2. Presence of good site like waterfalls, impermeable rock among others.
3. There should be reliable capital availability in order to invest all activities for establishing HEP station.
4. There should be technological advancement in order to run the project.

Importance of Hydroelectric Power:

1. Stimulates development of industries.
2. Encourages environmental conservation since it reduces the demand of the forest for power.

3. It encourages development of agricultural sector, tourism and mining sector.
4. It promotes the living standard of people.
5. HEP can be exported to other countries and bring in some foreign currency.
6. It encourages the development of science and technology, especially in the communication system like internet service.

Problems Encountered in Harnessing HEP

The following are the problems encountered in harnessing hydroelectric power:

1. Seasonal fluctuation in the volume of the river which makes it difficult to turn the turbines.
2. Excessive evaporation of water, leads to the reduction of water.
3. Underground percolation of water in sources of water.
4. Poor capital availability for constructing dams.
5. Inadequate availability of skilled labor like engineers and technicians.
6. Poor market, especially where the industrial base is poor.
7. Lack of communication network to link the area of production and the area of consumption.
8. Silting of dams which lead to the reduction in the volumes of water.
9. Lack of appropriate technology among the people in the country.
10. Destruction of power lines or transmission cables due to the results of civil wars and people steal some of the cable.

River Basin Development (Wetland Development Projects)

River basin is the land that is drained by a river and its tributaries. River basin development is therefore the sustainable use of river basin resources of economic gains and river basin development projects are schemes which are developed for different purposes.

Examples of river basin projects:

Africa: Volta river project (Ghana) Orange river project (S. Africa), Gezira irrigation scheme (Sudan), Aswan high dam (Egypt), Mwea-Tebere and Galde irrigation scheme in Kenya, Rufiji basin development, Kilombelo basin development and Kagera river basin development scheme (Tanzania).

Other River Basin Out Of Africa: Tennessee valley project (USA), Indus (Pakistan) Gouges project (India), Amazon basin development scheme (Brazil).

Process in the River Basin Development:

1. Construction of the dams for retaining water.
2. Dredging of the river. This refers to the removed of, straightening, and deepening and remove of silt or mud from the river so that it can accommodate more water.
3. Clearing of vegetation where economic activities are going to take place
4. Planting of tree on the sides of the river so as to protect soil erosion and preventing flooding due to the surface run-off of water.
5. Creating some canals and installing the pipes that can help irrigation.

Conditions in Order a River Basin Development to Take Place:

1. The river basin has to cover a substantially large area.
2. The volume of the main river and its tributaries have to be large
3. The impact of the development should not negatively affect the people in the locality or the ecosystem.
4. There should be adequate funds to ensure successfully development.
5. Availability of land to set up offices and other necessary building and facilities.

Economic Importance (Benefits) of River Basin Development

The following are the economic importance of river basin development:

(1) River basin development helps in the control of floods where they are established.

(2) Lead to the improvement of navigation in the respective rivers where dams are constructed.

(3) Lead to the development of fishing activities.

(4) Ensure the availability of water supply to the domestic uses, and industrial uses.

(5) Helps to develop irrigation scheme leading to the development of agriculture.

(6) River development projects encourages the protection of the environment because there are planted trees.

(7) Act as the source of employment to the people corresponding to the respective locality.

(8) They lead to the development of timber industry like in Sweden; logs are transported in down streams to saw mills.

(9) Silt removed from the river during dredging add humans to the soil and hence promotes farming.

(10) Acts as Centre for HEP generation.

(11) River basin encouraged the development of towns in many countries, like Germany (Cologne, Bonn and frankfurt).

(12) Used as research centers for studying ecosystems and their importance to human being.

(13) River basin development encourages development of tourism since dams are used as recreational centers gorges and water falls for viewing hence source of foreign currency to the country.

Setbacks or Hindrances of River Basins (Wetlands) Development Projects

There following are the problems, challenges or limitation facing river basin development:

1. Unreliable rainfall and excessive evaporation lead to the dry of rivers and other water bodies.
2. Accumulations of silt in the dams lead to the reduction of the volume of water.
3. Water pollution especially by the industries discourages the utilization of water from the river basin projects.
4. Lack of capital for establishing and maintaining the river basin projects.
5. Soil exhaustion due to intensive farming.
6. The outbreak of disease like malaria and cholera.
7. There is a problem of displacing the people to other areas in establishing the project.
8. Soil erosion can also affect the established river basin development.
9. Flooding due to high volume of water that caused by rainfall and melting of ice.

Rufiji Basin Development Authority (RU.BA.D.A)

River Rufiji is the largest river in Tanzania. It starts in the Southern highlands and has many tributaries such as the Great Ruaha River and ends in the Indian Ocean. The Rufiji river basin covers mainly the regions of coast, Morogoro,

Mbeya, Iringa and some parts of Dodoma and Ruvuma. It has different resources including water, oil, natural gas, flora and fauna and land that is fertile.

Some of the main economic activities carried out within the basin include agriculture (farming), hydroelectric power production, irrigation, fishing and navigation. The Rufiji basin development authority (RUBADA) is a project which was set in 1975 to oversee the development of the Rufiji River Basin.

Benefits of the Rufiji Basin Development Authority:
1. A hydropower plant such as Kidatu which generates electricity.
2. HEP Produced by RUBADA help in the development of industries in the country.
3. The authority has encouraged the promotion, growth and development of tourism in the river basin. The Selous, Ruangwa and Ruaha national parks are example of the tourism attractions that located to the basin.
4. The development of Rufiji basin lead to the creation of job opportunities like in RUBADA and economic activities that are taking place in the river basin.
5. Facilitates to the improvement of agriculture, due to the presence of water for irrigation.
6. RUBADA ensured the environmental conservation in any activities operated within the basin development.
7. Act as the source of foods both aquatic food and agricultural food.
8. Encourages on the development of water supply to the home steady and industries.

Problems facing Rufiji Basin Development Authority:
1. Inadequate capital.
2. Low level of technology.
3. Rural-urban migration. This has denied the authority the necessary skilled and unskilled labors required to carry out developmental activities.
4. Poor transport and communication infrastructure.
5. Lack of support by local communities. Some of the local communities do not support some of the activities carried out or proposed by RUBADA.

6. Fluctuations of water levels. This is due to the variation of seasons especially summer and winter season.

Prospects of the Authority

The RUBADA has great power for growth. This potential will only be realized if the authority can put together large amounts of capital and receive great support from the government and the local communities. Below is an outline of potentials:

1. *Hydroelectric power generation:* If funds are available, the authority will be able to upgrade its power production and setting new stations for power production.

2. *Transport:* The authority is yet to actually exploit the potential of transport activities in the Basin. Navigation in this Basin is poor, but through introduction of better water vessels will improve transport in the area.

3. *Fisheries:* Fishing in the basin is still on a very small scale. There is a great potential for fisheries in this region. Fish farms may also be set up to commercially produced for sale.

4. *Forestry:* The authority has noted that, there is great potential for development and exploitation of forest resources in the basin at the industrial level. With adequate finances, the authority will be able to invest in this area and get good returns.

5. *Tourism:* The Selous game reserve has one of the largest mammal populations in the world. It also has unique plant species. This makes it quite suitable for eco-tourism; these entire if observed clearly the basin would be great with potential for development.

6. *Agriculture:* The total irrigable land in the basin is more than 620, 000 ha. Only a very small part of this land can be brought under irrigation. More agricultural production in the area can be highly attained.

Tennessee Valley Authority (TVA)

The Tennessee valley refers to the drainage basin of the Tennessee River in USA. Tennessee is the tributary of Ohio River in the United States of America (USA). The Ohio River is in turn the tributary of the Mississippi river. The valley is much known in the world in terms of successful controlling the problem of severe soil erosion.

The Basin is spread across the states of Tennessee, Alabama, North Carolina, Kentucky, Georgia, Mississippi and Virginia. Some of the rivers in the basin include Holston River, Watauga River, Tennessee River and Doe River. The basin also has the Great Smoky Mountains and the Cumberland Plateau. The Tennessee valley Authority (TVA), Created in 1933, is a fully government owned body in charge of development activities in this Basin.

Aims of the Scheme Authority:
1. To control soil erosion and improve the quality of the land that had been degraded by severe soil erosion.
2. To control the floods.
3. To improve navigation.
4. To develop hydroelectric power generation centers.
5. Agricultural improvement.

Achievements of the Authority or Scheme:
1. Generation of electricity.
2. Successful control of soil erosion.
3. To control flood.
4. To improve navigation.

Steps that TVA took in developing the valley:
a) Constructing the dams along the river course.
b) Reforestation was done especially on the steep slopes of Appalachian Mountains.
c) Gullies were filled up with brushwood to trap the eroded soil particles especially silt.
d) Modern farming methods were introduced, for example terracing, contour ploughing and crop rotation on the slopes.
e) Planting of grass or cover crops on the slopes so as to reduce surface run off.

Benefits of the TVA:

a) The authority has successfully managed to curb soil erosion.

b) The construction of dams and planting trees among other measure has helped to control flooding in the valley.

c) Through irrigation the authority has managed to increase agriculture production.

d) Ensured the supply of electricity the industries and homes in the basin.

e) Ensure water supply both to the domestic uses and industrial uses.

f) Availability of abundant water supply and electricity, the authority has attracted many investors is aluminum smeltry, that led to industrialization in the area.

g) The activities in the authority created job opportunities to the people.

h) Navigation in the basin has improved transportation of goods and people around the area of the basin.

i) Development of fishing industries.

Qn: Discussion for the results of TVA project in the USA

Prospects of the Tennessee Valley Authority

Despite the success, so far achieved by TVA, there is still great potential for further development. The following are some of the prospects:

1. There is still great room for the expansion of gain culture in the region. There is still a lot of arable land and irrigable land that has not been fully utilizes.

2. A lot of land is still available for the establishment of various industries. Potential growth areas include car manufacturing and textile manufacturing.

3. The TVA has a lot of potential in the power generation sector. The main potential lies in generation of nuclear power.

Land Reclamation

Land reclamation refers to efforts to make land that was previously unproductive to be useful. It is the process of turning the waste (poor) land into a useful state. Land reclamation is also defined as the process of converting wasteland into land that can be used for economic activities and settlement.

Aims of Land Reclamation:

1. To increase the size land for agriculture.
2. To add the size of land available for human settlement.
3. To make availability of more land for the establishment of industries and offices.
4. To be in proximity to resources in order to be able to gain fully utilization of them.

Main Four Land Reclamation Techniques
The techniques used to reclaim land depend on the status of the land:

1. Irrigation: This refers to the activities of supplying water to dry areas. This is done through use of simple, pumps, pipes, or sometimes by constructing dams along rivers to create water reservoirs.

2. Afforestation: This refers to the establishment of forests water they did not previously existed. This carried out the area that experiencing desert condition and high rates of soil erosion. Afforestation is done for four (4) major reasons:
   a) To create water catchments.
   b) To protect the soil from erosion.
   c) Forest may be established for commercial purposes:
      ↳ Extraction of timber
      ↳ To provide wood pulp for to manufacture paper.
   (a) Forest has been known to modify the climate of an area.

3. Drainage: This is the process of reclaiming land that has stagnant water; example, sea water and other sources of water so as to: *(a) avoid flooding (b) to get area for agriculture etc*. A good example is in Zuider Zee project in the Netherland.

4. Cleaning vegetation and controlling pests: Some areas can be reclaimed due to the dense vegetation covers in order to clear pests (e.g. tsetse flies). Sterilization may also be used to control pests away from the uses of pesticides.

How Land Reclamation is done in The Country like Tanzania?
Various efforts have been made to reclaim wasteland in Tanzania. Some of the efforts include the followings:

1. Irrigation: This has been carried out in the dry lands found within the Rufiji basin through using water from Rufiji basin for irrigation purposes.

2. Drainage: Parts of Dodoma and Dar es Salaam have been reclaimed through this method, especially in the area of Kunduchi and Msasani. Most of this land was reclaimed for settlement purposes.

3. Afforestation and Agroforestry: This is one of the most used methods of land reclamation in Tanzania. Example; in Shinyanga region that was reclaimed through afforestation that programmed and called Hifadhi Ardhi Shinyanga (HASHI). Also in Dodoma at Kondoa District, land also has been reclaimed through afforestation due to severe erosion.

4. Clearing of vegetation: This was mainly done by the colonialists especially in the Miombo woodlands. This was done in order to make the land useful for livestock keeping, settlement and crop cultivation.

Sustainable Use of Water Resources

Water is found both at the surface of the earth and underground. Underground water also called ground water or subterranean water or phreatic water. Underground water is the water that found below the surface of the earth. *Sustainable use of water resources* refers to the proper use of water resource in relation to the protection of water sources.

Underground water

Underground water is water that found beneath or under the earth's surface. There are main five types of underground water, which are explained below:

1. Rain water or meteoric water: This are water that formed when rainfalls on the ground (are underground water that originated from rainfall), then water enter (infiltrates) the ground through the available cracks and pores in soil.

2. Melt water: Is the underground water that formed in the areas that experienced in the winter season, snow accumulates on the ground during cold period. Also melt water enter the ground as rainwater does.

3. Connate water: Is water that was retained within the sedimentary rocks since the time of their formation. Most of connate water is saline.

4. Magnetic or juvenile or plutonic water: This is water that gets trapped in the rocks beneath the surface during volcanism (volcanic activities). Magnetic water contains a lot of mineral and is usually hot.

5. Oceanic water: This is underground water that results from seepage of ocean water into the ground. This water inters the ground seepage through the available spaces.

Ways used to tap underground water
The following are the ways in which underground water can be taped:

1. *Drilling boreholes:* Holes are dug deep into the ground until the underground water is reached. The water is then pumped to surface and collected through taps.

2. *Digging wells:* A hole is dug into the ground until the water is reached.

Note: The difference between wells and boreholes is, the water from wells is fetched manually or through use of simple pulley. The wall of well may also be lined with bricks or stone and cement.

3. *Where the water occurs close to the surface:* Can be scooped to expose the water. Can be scooped using cups or other utensils. Can also water be directed to farms for irrigation through use of channel or pumped into lines.

4. *Natural springs or oases:* Underground water can be naturally exposed to form springs or oases in deserts. This water may be directly scooped using various utensils or containers. Also may be directed to farms through channels.

Resources Obtained from Water
The following are some of the resources obtained from water sources:

   1. Fishes and other edibles water creatures, such as prawn, which is used for food.

   2. Sand, which is used in building.

   3. Hydropower, which is used to generate electricity.

4. Salt, which is used domestically as well as in industries.
5. Decorative items such as cowries' shells.

Extraction of water resources

Extraction of water resource is the process of getting resources from all water bodies. Water resources can be extracted as follows:

1. Fish and other edible water creatures: Fish may be obtained from water through use of hooks and line, nets, herbs, spears, or traps. Hooks are used for small scale fishing unlike to the use of nets.

2. Sand: This is harvested by dredging riverbeds or riverbanks. This may be done by using scooping machine or by hand using simple pans.

3. Salt: Salt is acquired mainly through evaporation. Salty water is trapped in ponds. Due to rapid evaporation of water caused by high temperatures, salt crystals are left behind in the ponds. These crystals are collected and processed. Alternative methods are where the salty water is pumped into evaporation tanks from where the evaporation is conducted.

4. Hydropower: Hydropower is tapped by directing the water to turn turbines, which are used to generate electricity.

5. Decorative items: This can be harvested from the sea floor or beaches by simply picking them up. There is no specialized process of obtaining them.

Problems Caused by Extraction of Water Resources:

1. Over fishing and indiscriminate fishing in which even immature fish are caught reduces the availability of fish. It causes an imbalance in the eco-system.

2. Sand harvesting may lead to loss of soil for growth of plant life in the water bodies.

3. Hydropower harvesting may cut-off water supply to the area due to the construction of dams.

4. Construction of dams in harvesting hydroelectric power, may lead to the breeding of snails and mosquitoes that cause bilharzias and malaria respectively.

Solutions to the Problems Caused By the Extraction of Water Resources:

1. Monitoring the nets used by fishermen to ensure that the net holes are too small that has not to catch young and immature fish.

2. Restricting fishing in some areas to allow fish to breed and increase in number.

3. Encouraging people to practice fish farming so as to reduce pressure on natural water bodies such as rivers and lakes.

4. Restricting or controlling sand harvesting to ensure that aquatic life is no not destroyed or interfered with.

Water Pollution

Water pollution refers to the introduction of harmful substances into water bodies or sources. Pollution refers to the introduction of harmful substances into the environment. Water pollution kills aquatic life and renders the water unfit for human consumption or for any other productive uses.

Source of water pollution

The followings are the main sources of water pollution:

1. Industrial waste: Industrial wastes are gases, oil, and chemical as well as solid waste such as scrap metals. This waste is either released directly into water sources or dumped onto land from where it is washed into water sources.

2. Domestic waste: This includes sewage, dirty water used for washing, food remains, dead animals, plastics and insecticides. This also may be dumped directly into the water sources or dumped on land and washed into the water sources by running rainwater.

3. Agricultural chemicals: These include insecticides, fertilizers, pesticides and herbicides, which are chemicals used for agricultural purposes. These chemicals may be good to use on land but when they are washed into water sources, they tend to pollute the water sources.

4. *Oil spills:* Oil spills normally occur in oceans during transportation of oil. The spill may be caused by a leakage in the pipelines or due to damage or sinking of ships carrying the oil.

5. *Extensive construction:* Large building and construction projects may lead to water pollution. Soil dug during the construction may be washed off into water sources. Materials such as cement may also be washed into the water sources, thus polluting the water.

Water Conservation

Water conservation refers to the protection of water and water sources. We can conserve water in the following ways:

1. *Avoiding wastage:* People should avoid wasting water. They should be encouraged to use water sparingly. People should turn off taps every time when are not using.

2. *Controlling pollution:* The control of water pollution starts with the individual. We should each ensure that we do dump waste or threw litters carelessly because it may end up being washed into water sources and pollute them.

3. *Enforcement of law:* Strictly laws should be encouraged and enforced to discourage industries as well as individual from discharging their waste into water sources.

4. *Protection of water catchments:* The government should ensure that human activities in water catchments do not interfere water catchments.

5. *Education:* People should be educated on the importance of conserving water resources.

6. *Sewage treatment:* Sewage effluent should be treated before it is released into the water bodies. This reduces the level of pollution.

7. Controlled use of agricultural chemicals: The use of chemicals in farms should be controlled, especially in areas that border water bodies.

8. Recycling: People should be encouraged to recycle their waste rather than dumping it. People can recycle water, plastics bags, scrap metal and glass, among many other possible pollutants.

9. Immediate clean up: In case of oil spills immediate and thorough clearing of the water should be done. This can be done by use of chemicals and special machines called skimmer ships.

TRIAL QUESTIONS

1. List down four domestic uses of water.

2. Show how water is important in economic development of the country.

3. Mention three sources of water in your place you live.

4. Identify the problems of water supply in the country.

5. Suggest the ways of solving the problems of water supply in any country.

6. How does the shortage of water affect the society of Africa?

7. Show the role of vegetation in the supply of water.

8. List down the factors that affects water supply in the countries of East Africa.

9. Explain in point form about how the distance of water sources affects girl children in Africa.

10. Define water management and water conservation.

11. Why should water be conserved?

12. Identify ways that can be used in conserving the water sources in your country.

13. What are the advantages of the river basin development schemes?

14. Mention five disadvantages of river basin development schemes in Africa.

15. Mention six river basin development schemes in Africa.

16. What are the basic requirements for developing the river basin development?

17. Outline the factors that facilitate the development of river basin development.

18. Mention the factors that hinder the development of river development schemes.

19. List down the problems caused by river basin development scheme.

20. Show five achievements of the TVA attained in development of Tennessee valley.

21. Explain four benefits of the farmers get from the river basin development.

22. (a) What is land reclamation?

(b) Identify the process (techniques) which were involved in land reclamation in Tanzania

(c) Mention 4 advantages of land reclamation in Tanzania.

(d) Describe how the reclaimed land is used in Tanzania.

23. Mention the factors that hinder land reclamation in any country you have studied.

24. Define underground water and mention its three types.

25. Mention five problems (factors) that hinder Tanzania from utilizing the underground water properly.

26. Briefly explain the relationship between water supply and quality of life. Give clear example.

27. What are some of the developments that have taken place in Rufiji river basin?

28. State five water resources, and explain how each one is extracted.

29. Explain three problems resulting from the harvesting of water resources and finally suggest solutions to the problems.

30. What are the economic importance? Give five reasons.

CHAPTER 04:

SUSTAINABLE USE OF FOREST RESOURCES

Forest refers to the collection of trees, which can be natural or artificial. There are main two types of forests as namely: *natural forests* and *artificial forests*. *Natural forests,* these are forests developed without the influence and input of human beings while *planted* or *artificial forests* are forests that developed when the human beings plant trees on large piece of land.

Main Characteristics of natural forests:
1. Trees of different types grown together.
2. Most of the trees produce hardwood.
3. The trees in the forest are indigenous to the area.
4. There is dense or thick undergrowth.

Main Characteristics of planted forests:
1. Trees are mainly of one species.
2. Trees may or may not be indigenous to the area.
3. Are in specific lines.
4. Most of trees in this category produce softwood.

Division of natural forests
Natural forest can be divided basing on the climates as follow:

1. Tropical rain forests: These are found in the equatorial region. They are characterized by thick undergrowth, and very tall trees which are indigenous that take a very long time to mature.

2. Mangrove forests: Are forests that found along coastlines. Trees under this are having shallow roots and can tolerate salty conditions of seawater.

3. Temperate forests: Found in the hemispheres of the earth. They may be evergreen or deciduous (that is, the trees shed their leaves at the beginning of the cold season).

4. Coniferous forests: Are forests that found in outermost part of the earth's hemisphere. Evergreen trees with needle-like leaves, little undergrowth and all trees, which take very long to mature, characterize them.

Factors Influencing the Nature and Distribution of Forests:

1. Relief: Relief refers to the landscape, which is a physical feature on the earth's surface. Differences in altitude along the slope of mountain bring about differences in the type of forests along the mountain slope

2. Aspect: This is the direction of a slope faces with respect to sunshine and the rain-bearing winds. For example in temperate latitudes in the northern hemisphere where the sun's position is near over head at noon, the slopes facing south are warmer than the northward facing the slopes; therefore forests grow on the southward facing slopes more than on the north facing slopes.

3. Drainage: Well-drained soil support tree while poorly drained soil do not support the growth of trees.

4. Temperature: The warm or hot tropical climate support the growth of large trees with broad leaves while cooler temperate climate where snowfalls support conifer type of trees, which are adapted to that kind of climate. Conifer trees have thin leaves and are cone-shaped.

5. Rainfall: Water is very essential for plant growth. Forests thrive in area, which have high rainfall. Trees in some forests shed their leaves at the beginning of the dry season to reduce water loss through transpiration.

6. Soil or edaphic: Soil provides nutrients and anchorage to trees. Other soil characteristics such as acidity, organic and chemical composition determine the kind of tree growing in particular soil.

7. Human activities: People do influence in determining the distribution of forests. They can increase the size of forests by planting more trees to an existing forest or introduce new species in an area were non-before. On the other hand, people also destroy the existing forest by cutting down trees carelessly.

Importance of Forest Resources:

The following are ways in which forest resources seemed to be very important:

a) Forests are source of timber.
b) Forests are source of fuel woods and charcoals.
c) Forests protect the soil or land from being attacked by soil erosion.
d) Large variety soft wood trees are used for making pulps which are used in paper manufacturing.
e) Forests produce building materials like poles and timber.
f) Some of tree species are used for making medicine.
g) Some forests produce fruits and ornamental flowers.
h) They contribute to the soil development through rotting of leaves, which leads to formation of humus.
i) Forests are used for scientific study (research).
j) They maintain water sources.
k) Flora and fauna of forests act as tourism attraction.
l) Source of foreign currency, revenue and income.
m) Act as sources of employment.

Types of Forest Resources or Products:

a) Poles for building and construction of houses.
b) Timber for furniture, construction, railways slippers.
c) Resins, oil and gum.
d) Fiber material for different uses (for making loops, clothes etc.)
e) Fruit, nuts and flowers for human and animal consumption.
f) Tannin, which is obtained from the hemlock tree of North America and Europe. Oak and chest nut of temperate hardwood.
g) Palm and creeper products, such as, palm oil, coconuts, mat and basket weaving materials from palms and bamboo.
h) Medicinal materials such as, quinine from cinchona tree, cocaine from coca plants, camphor from the camphor tree.

Major Producers of Forest Products or Materials:

The followings are the world's leading countries in production of forest products:

No	Products	Leading producers/countries
01	Timber and wood fuels.	Russia, USA, Brazil, China, Canada, Indonesia, Japan, Sweden, Nigeria, France, Finland, Germany.

02	Timber from hard woods.	Indonesia, Brazil, China, USA, Russia, India, Nigeria, Tanzania, Malaysia, Philippines
03	Timber from soft woods.	Canada, USA, Russia, Japan, Finland, Sweden, China, Brazil, Germany,
04	Wood pulps.	Canada, Finland, Sweden, Japan, France, Germany, Norway, New Zealand, Brazil, China, USA, Russia.
05	Newsprints.	Canada, USA, Japan, Russia, Sweden, Finland, Germany, Norway, UK.
06	Rubber and gum	Brazil, Nigeria, USA, Indonesia.
07	Cork.	USA, Portugal, Spain, Morocco.
08	Resin, Tar, Turpentine	USA, Russia, France.

Problems Associated With Forest Resources Harvesting

The following are the problems associated with forest resources extraction:

1. Deforestation (felling of trees) exposes the soil to agents of soil erosion.
2. Forested areas are water catchment, over exploitations of forest resources leads to the destruction of these water catchment areas.
3. Cutting down trees without replanting new ones may cause climatic changes leading to drought and famine.
4. Reduction of forest cover leading to the increase of carbon dioxide in the atmosphere, hence leads to the greenhouse effect, which cause to global warming.
5. Uncontrolled tree harvesting interferes with the ecological balance of forest flora and fauna.
6. Rapid population growth has led to the clearance of forests in many places.
7. Poor capital in the developing countries.
8. Low technology leads to the use poor tools.
9. Stiff challenges posed by other economic sectors.

Measures for Forest Conservation in the World

There are number of measures that can be taken effectively to manage forests:

1. Creating public awareness. Through campaign using mass media, poster and provision of education to the people.

2. Carrying out research to determine the requirements for different tree species. This will ensure that, the right tree species is planted in the correct areas.

3. Encouraging the use of existing alternative sources of energy instead of relying on woods fuel and charcoals. Alternative sources are kerosene, solar energy, biomass to mention a few.

4. Enforcing rules about selective felling of trees and planting new ones to replace those are cut.

5. Enactment of laws, which can be used effectively to manage forests and manage them against destruction.

6. Others are: Application of afforestation and reafforestation. Population control so as to reduce pressure on the forest resources. Discouragement of poor agricultural methods that affects forests. Destocking should be also encouraged nearby forest reserves and new and fast growing of trees for timber production should be introduced.

Forest Resource Management

Forest resource management refers to the control and proper use of forest resources for different purposes. *Forest conservation* is the protection of forests resources. Forest management is the part of forestry. *Forestry* refers to the science of managing forest resources for human use. Another term that used in forest resource management is *Agro-forestry* which mean as the practice of intercropping trees and crops in the same farm.

Activity:
1. Discuss the needs of forest resources management.
2. Highlight for the effects of poor forest management.
3. Describe the advantages and disadvantages of intercropping trees with crops (agro-forest).

Timber Transportation

Timber transportation refers to the process of transporting timbers and logs from the forest area to the market. The logs are pulled by caterpillars or by tractor-driven trailer and Lorries out of the dense forests to the saw-mills. The sawn timbers are then transported by Lorries (trucks) and train to the market or port for export by ships. Movement of logs and timber from the forest to the market particularly poses great challenges.

TRIAL QUESTIONS

1. Define:

    a. Forest,

    b. Forestry,

    c. Agro forest,

    d. Forest resource management,

    e. Forest resource conservation,

    f. Afforestation and

    g. Reafforestation.

2. With the aid of examples, explain the importance of preserving forest.

3. Describe the disadvantages of deforestation (at least five points).

4. Explain the human factors, which lead to deforestation.

5. What do you understand by the term agro-forest?

6. Discuss the factors influencing the distribution of forests in the world.

7. Discuss the problems associated with exploitation or harvesting of forest resources.

8. Distinguish between:

    a)   Forest conservation and forest management.

    b) Afforestation and reafforestation.

9. Mention the main measures for preventing forests.

10. (i) List five measures that can be taken to manage forests.

    (ii) List two measures that can be taken to conserve forests.

CHAPTER 05:

MANUFACTURING INDUSTRY

Definition of Terms:

Manufacture is the situation of uses of machine to make goods or materials, usually in large number or amounts. *Manufacturing* is the process or business of producing goods in factories (also known as production). *Industry* is any form of economic activities in which people produce goods or provide services for their uses or sales.

Manufacturing industry is an industry that involves large scale of production of goods using machines. *Industrialization* refers to the establishment of industries in a country on a given area (alternatively; it is when the country develops many industries). An important note: Manufacturing industry also refers to the secondary industries; because, products of primary industries turn them into useful products.

Types of Manufacturing Industry

Manufacturing industries are involved in converting raw materials into semi processed or finished products. Therefore, manufacturing industries can be into two broad categories:

1. Processing industries
2. Fabrication industries.

1. Processing Industries: These are industries that use raw material from the primary industries and convert them into goods that can be used as raw materials. Examples of processing industries are cotton ginneries, coffee factories and sisal factories.

2. Fabrication Industries: Are industries that use raw materials from processing industries to come up with new products. Most of these industries use steels to make machinery.

Note: Sometimes, manufacturing industries are as *light (processing)t* and *heavy (fabrication)* industries:

1. Light industries: Involves in manufacturing products that are not bulky or heavy. Examples of light industries include food processing, printing, electronics, textile, plastic and cosmetics industries among others.

2. Heavy industries: Involves in manufacturing heavy and bulky products. These are made by using raw materials like iron and steel. Examples of heavy industries are car making industries and ship building industries among others.

Conditions for Location of Manufacturing Industries

Factors influencing or facilitating the location of manufacturing industries involves the decision to establish an industry in a particular place in depending a number of factors as follows:

1. Availability of raw materials. The presence of raw material is an important factor to the establishment of manufacturing industries in an area and in the country as well.

2. Availability of energy and power supply. Industries cannot be established without energy or power. The availability of power and energy in an area such as coals, petroleum and electricity tends to influence the manufacturing industries to be established in order to reduce the cost for transporting powers and energy to the industries.

3. Presence of labor or man power. Human resource is an important factor in the location of industries. Manufacturing Industries needs skilled and unskilled workers to support the works in industries.

4. Availability of capital. A lot of money is needed in the investment of manufacturing industries, like money for establishing infrastructures, importing raw materials, payment for workers among others.

5. Presence of market. Availability of market close to the industry may cut for costs of transportation from industrial areas to the market areas; hence, an industry can be established.

6. Presence of transport and communication. The industrial area must be well linked with transport and communication system from the source of raw materials, to the industrial area as well as to the market area by road, railways, ports and communication networks.

7. Government support. Government policies and supports play a big role in influencing the establishment of manufacturing industries. The government support and encouragement may facilitate for the concentration of industries in an area. Government support can be provision of loans, security, incentives, services, and infrastructure to the industrial owners.

8. Availability of water Supply. Most of industries needs lot amount of water in their operations, like cooling machines, washing raw material and in making ingredients in various products, hence, constant water supply is required.

9. Industrial inertia and historical factors. The tendency of old industries where they are located even when the factors favoring their location are no longer important (this is referred as industrial inertia). In addition, this may be due to reason such as availability of skilled and experienced labor, well-developed transport and communication networks and the fear for the expenses may be incurred in moving to the new place.

Factors Limiting for the Establishment of Manufacturing Industries
The followings are factors or reasons hindering for establishment of manufacturing industries:
Lack of capital, poor government support, shortage of skilled labor, poor transport and communication system, high competition in markets, poor water supply, poor energy and power supply, high competition from other economic sectors, such as mining, challenges from environmentalists on the issue of environmental protection and shortage of raw materials.

Importance of Manufacturing Industry
Manufacturing industry contributes to the economic growth and development of a country. Manufacturing industry is important in the following some of reasons:

Act as source of employment: When manufacturing industries are established, they require people to work in them, hence act as the source of employment to the people in the country.

A source of foreign currency (foreign exchange): The products that are manufactured in a country are exported to other countries, and this generates foreign currency in the country.

It stimulates the development of infrastructures: Industries require proper transport and communication infrastructure to function well, hence led to the development of infrastructures like roads, railways, and water and airways.

It leads to the development of agricultural production: Most of manufacturing industries obtain raw materials from agricultural production in order to manufacture readymade goods, hence facilitate for the increase of agricultural production.

Improve international relations: Production from manufacturing industries improves international relations through international trades that make interaction among the people of different countries and continents.

Reduces dependence on imports: A country that is well developed in manufacturing industries is able to meet the needs of its people, hence may reduce dependence on importation from other countries.

It encourages to the improvements of social services: Social services like water supply, power and energy supply, education and health services.

Encourages on the exploitation of resources: Manufacturing industries needs natural resources like minerals, materials from forest and water to make readmade goods that ready to be used, hence may encourage on the exploitation of natural resource.

Negative Impacts or Effects of Manufacturing Industry:
Manufacturing industries have the following effects, both on environmental, economic and social aspects:

Lead to land degradation: This is because on clearing the forest for establishing industries and extraction of raw materials and natural resources on the land.

Cause for environmental pollution: This is through air pollution, water pollution, land pollution and noise pollution, through emission of chemicals, smokes, and waste disposal that pollute the environment.

Lead to the occurrence of diseases: These diseases are due to pollution on the environment that caused by industries. Pollution of water may lead for water borne diseases like typhoid, diarrhea and cancer. Air pollution may cause for diseases like Tuberculosis (TB) and bronchitis; while noise pollution may cause for disease like mental problems and stress.

Decline of other economic activities: This is due to the fact that, people and the government may involve much on manufacturing industries, hence other economic activities like tourism, lumbering, to mention a few, may decline.

Cause for overpopulation: Development of manufacturing industries may cause for the overpopulation in an area, hence may lead for the eruption of communicable diseases, increase of crimes, shortage of food and social services.

Industrial Pollutants

Pollutants are substances that make air, water, soil (environment) to be harmful or polluted. Industrial pollutants are substances that produced by factories that cause pollution on the environment. Pollutants from industries are into four types that are namely below:

1. Gases pollutants: Industrial activities results on the emission of harmful smokes and gases into the atmosphere. Such gases include sulphur dioxide, carbon dioxide, carbon monoxide, nitrogen oxide, and other hydrocarbons.

2. Particulates or particles: Sometimes industries emit harmful particles, into the environment in the course of their activities. These particles include dust particles, pieces of glass and plastics among others.

3. Noise: Noise is a loud, unwanted and disturbing sound. Most of industries produce a lot of noise from the machines they use.

4. Liquid: Liquid pollutants are all harmful fluid. Emitted harmful liquids from manufacturing industries are; sewage oils, toxic chemicals among others.

Ways which can be used to Reduce Industrial Pollution

The following are the ways in which can be used to reduce industrial pollution:

1. Industries should be allocated away from residential areas.
2. Recycling of industrial waste materials should be encouraged.
3. Complete combustion of fuels in industrial machines should be observed.
4. Industrial wastes should be well lubricated to reduce noise pollution.
5. There should be establishment and enforcement of proper rules and law to guide industrial owners on how to treat and dispose of the various wastes.
6. There should be other activities developed to avoid over dependency on manufacturing industries only.
7. Environmental Impact Assessment (E.I.A) should be carried out before establishing manufacturing industries.

Types of Manufacturing Industries that are found in East Africa

There are different types of manufacturing industries in East Africa. They can be grouped as:

1. Energy and power industries: These industries deal with generation of electricity e.g. Hydroelectric Power (HEP) as well as extraction of gas and refining of oil.

2. Metal Industries: Metal industries, are industries that are involved in the production of finished products from iron and steel. Examples of these industries are those, which manufacture iron sheets for roofing.

3. Lumbering industries: These are industries produce timber, wood, pulp, and other materials from like papers.

4. Food processing industry: These are most common among the East African countries. They process agricultural products and produce into other new products.

5. Textile industries: They process fibers from cotton, wool and other fibers into finished products such as clothes. Examples of textile industries are Mwatex, Kilitex, and Sunguratex.

6. Chemical industries: These industries produce products by using mixture of chemicals. Examples of products produced by these industries are; soaps, fertilizers, toothpaste, and plastics.

7. Tobacco processing and cigarettes making industries: In Tanzania there are several tobacco processing and cigarettes making industries mostly located in Dar es Salaam.

Cars Production in Japan

Japan is an island country that found in the part of East Asian continent. Japan is made up by islands like Honshu, Hokkaido, Shikoku among others. Japan is among of the industrialized countries in the world. It is also among of the leading countries in manufacturing cars like Toyota, Isuzu, Suzuki and Mitsubishi as well as auto car parts.

Factors Influencing for the Growth of Cars Manufacturing in Japan

The growth of car manufacturing in Japan has been influenced by the following factors:

    a) Technological development.
    b) Adequate capital.
    c) Market availability
    d) Availability of manpower or labor
    e) Good infrastructure.
    f) High degree of government support.

Production of Electronic Equipment in South Korea

South Korea is located in Eastern Asia. South Korea produces electronic equipment like television, iron, watches, radios, memory cheeps (memory cards), calculator, and video players. Most of the leading companies that produce electronic equipment than others are: LG, and Samsung.

Factors which have led to the development and growth of South Korean's electronic equipment industry:

    1. Adequate capital.
    2. Availability of labor.
    3. Advancement of technology.
    4. Government support.
    5. International relations.

6. Well-developed infrastructure.
7. Availability of energy.

Industries in Tanzania

Textile industries in Tanzania developed in the year of 1970's by the effort of the government. However, with the liberalization of the economy in 1990's, led to the collapse of textile industry such as Mwanza textile industries, Musoma textile industries, and those survived operated at minimal production capacities.

The Tanzanian government has made a big effort to revive the textile sectors through privatization, joint venture and encouraging investment by reducing duty of paying tax, simplifying export procedure and relaxing exchange controls.

Problems Facing Textile Industry in Tanzania:
1. Outdated machinery.
2. High cost of spare parts.
3. Lack of personnel.
4. High competition from second hand clothes (called mitumba)
5. High taxes.
6. Lack of capital.
7. Poor infrastructure.
8. Poor management and administration.
9. High cost of chemicals that are used in color mixing.

Ways to be done in Order to Encourage Development of Textile Industries in Tanzania:
1. The government should support the textile industries financially.
2. There is a need for the textile industries to be up to date in terms of technology.
3. Market research should be a conducted into development of new products that give an edge to the textile industries.
4. There should be improvements of transport and communication.
5. The government should come up with reasonable policies for the textile industries.
6. There is a need to train enough labor related technical expertise in textile industry.
7. There should be an improvement of textile industries.

Lessons Tanzania Learn from Japan and South Korea's Industries

The following are some of the reasons in which Tanzania have to take a lesson from Japan and South Korean's industries:

1. Manufacturing industries in South Korea and Japan are well managed. This is the lesson to Tanzania industries.

2. The well-developed transport and communication in South Korea and Japan play the big role in development of industries. Through this, also Tanzania should develop its transport and communication infrastructure, so as textile industries and other industries to develop.

3. Japan and South Korean's industries have developed because of emphasis or research. The Tanzania textile industries should therefore carry out research in order to improve their products and methods of production.

4. The spirit of commitment and hard work played a major role in the industrial development of Japan and South Korea. Also, Tanzania should encourage commitment and hard working in its industries.

5. Tanzania should produce high quality products in its industries as Japan and South Korea does.

6. Tanzania should keep up to date its industries as Japan and South Korea do, to keep up with technological advancement.

7. Japan and South Korea exploit different resources of energy, making power cheap and reading available. Tanzania should follow this example and exploit various sources of power and energy rather than depending on hydroelectricity. This will make energy and power more cheap and available to industries.

TRIAL QUESTIONS

1. Define the following terms:
   a) Pollution

b) Industry

c) Manufacture

d) Manufacturing industry

e) Industrialization

2. In what ways is the manufacturing industry is very important to Tanzania.

3. (a) Name the types of industrial pollution.

(b) State four ways of reducing pollution from industries.

4. Explain for the impacts of manufacturing industries on the environment.

5. What are sources of industrial pollutants and how industrial pollutants affects environment and people as well.

6. Highlight five points on the factors influencing location of manufacturing industries.

7. Write short notes on the types of manufacturing industries.

8. Discuss for the factors influenced for growth of cars (automobile) manufacturing industry in Japan.

9. Describe the problems facing textile industries in Tanzania and ways to be used to alleviate such problems.

10. Which lessons may Tanzania learn from South Korean's electronic equipment industry?

CHAPTER 06:

TOURISM

Tourism is defined as the movement of people from one place to another either for studies, pleasure, leisure or business. The scope of tourism is regarded as social, cultural, political and economic aspects or activities. There are two main types of tourism:

      (a) Domestic tourism.
      (b) International tourism.

(a) Domestic tourism: It is the type of tourism that involves the movement of people from one place to another within a country. This can be from Mwanza to Lindi, or New York to California as an example.

(b) Interaction tourism: Is the type of tourism that refers to the movement of people from one country to another country or one continent to another continent. This can be from Tanzania to Kenya, Switzerland to Indonesia or Africa to Europe, Australia to North America and so forth.

Factors Influencing the Development of Tourism

These factors can both be political, social, culture and economic factors. The following are some of the factors that encourage the development of tourism in any country:

1. Present of Good climatic conditions: Good climatic conditions in a particular area may influence for the development of tourism.

2. Availability of attractive scenery: The presence of attractive landscapes or scenery also may influence for the development of tourism in a particular country.

3. Presence of historical sites: Also historical sites may attract tourists hence development of tourism in the country. Example of historical site is Kondoa Irangi in Tanzania.

4. Presence of national parks: Availability of national parks in the country also act as the factor for the development of tourism because, national parks tend to influence and attract for the visit of tourists in such area. Example of national park is Ngorongoro in Tanzania.

5. Availability of capital: Presence of enough capital that can be used for investment in tourism industry also is the factor that can influence for the development of tourism industry in the country.

6. Political stability: Presence of peace in the country may attract and influence tourists from different areas to visit a particular country. Absence of civil wars, tribal wars, religion wars and terrorism in the country may influence for the development of tourism.

7. Supportive government policy: If there is government policy that encourages tourism development in the country, may influence for the development 0f tourism in the particular country.

8. Advancement of transport and communication: In addition, the availability of good transport and communication in the country tend to encourage high number of tourists to inflow in the country.

9. Presence of accommodation facilities: These accommodations facilities like hotel, lodge and guest house are one among of the factors that influence for development of tourism in any country. These accommodations facilitate and ensure tourists to get places for leisure, pleasure and rest to the touristic areas.

General Importance of Tourism
Tourism industry has the following importance in any country in the world:

(1) *Tourism is the source of employment.* Tourism industry acts as the source of employment to the people in the country.

(2) *Tourism is the source of foreign currencies.* Tourism industry acts as the source of foreign currencies in any country, which are used by the go averment for exportation of products and raw materials.

(3) *It led to the improvement of infrastructure.* Tourism influence for the improvement transport system in the country.

(4) *Tourism is important in facilitating the improvement of social services.* Sources services like hospitals, school are improved due to the development of tourism industry, because all money earned by the government can be invested in the provision of social services.

(5) *It strengthens international relation among the country.* This is through movement of people or tourists from one country to another hence, development of international relations among the people of countries.

(6) *It promote for the rapid improvement of science and technology in the country.* This is due to the interaction of the people that provides chance for technological diffusion between the people in the country and tourists.

(7) *Tourism promoted for the development of other economic sectors.* Like agriculture, trade and exhibition.

(8) *Tourism facilitate for the environmental conservation.* Nation parks, nation reserves, historical sites and other sceneries that act as touristic attraction tend to be proper protected hence, improvement of environmental conservation.

(9) *Tourism acts as source of government revenue.* The governments in a particular country earn revenues in different way in the tourism in industry.

Impacts of Tourism

Tourism has positive and negative impacts in the world (any country in the world). The following are some of them:

Positive Impacts of Tourism

In the side of positive impacts of tourism, you can use those points from the importance of tourism in any country in the world.

Negative Impact of Tourism

The following are some of the negative effects or disadvantage of tourism industry in any country:

1. *Tourism discourage for the development of other economic activities*, like mining, Lumbering.

2. *Tourism leads to the destruction of culture.* For example, Most of Africa cultures are destructed by western culture due to the high interaction of people that caused by tourism industry.

3. *Tourism leads to the environmental destruction and soil erosion.* This is due to the frequent movement of cars and people to the touristic areas.

4. *Tourism influences the spread of diseases.* Tourisms may influence the spread of spread of dieses both sexual and communicable diseases. Tourists may spread diseases both sexual transmitted diseases (STDs) and other communicable disease like TB and Ebola. Example of STD is HIV/AIDS.

5. *Tourism cause to the overpopulation in an area.* Touristic area tends to be overpopulation because these areas attract many people in touristic centers.

6. *Running tourism industry, it is very expensive.* Tourism industry needs huge capital to be invested, hence may cause to the decline of other economic sectors.

7. *Facilitate to the increase of crime.* This is due to the moral decay and improper behavior caused by high number of people around touristic and the use of illegal ways of getting money through robbery and stealing visitors or tourists.

8. *Cause for the moral decay to the indigenous.* This is due to the destruction of natives' culture and adaptation or imitation of risk behavior from to the visitors or tourists.

Ways to be used so as to solve the negative impacts of tourism

The following are to the some of the solution to the negative impacts caused by tourism industry:

(a) Visitors or tourists must be taught the culture of the natives in order to avoid cultural interference or destruction.

(b) Reducing the number of visitors and natives in order to conserve the environment.

(c) There should be the enforcement of laws and strong security to the touristic centers in order to avoid crimes.

(d) The government should enforce laws that may lead to the protection from spread of diseases. For example, every tourist or visitors should be checked his or her health condition to testify that she or he is not affected by any disease.

(e) Natives should be given education to practice other economic activities instead of depending on tourism industry as the source of income.

(f) The government should not much invest on tourism industry rather than other economic sector and social services.

Green Tourism or Eco-Tourism

Green tourism or eco-tourism is defined as the integrated approach that involves carrying out tourism activities with minimum negative impact on the natural environmental. Green tourism improves the integration of tourism with ecology (ecosystem)

Case Study: Tourism in Switzerland

Switzerland is located at the central Europe. Areas mostly visited are the Swiss plateaus (of Lausanne, Geneva, Bern, and Zurich), Lakeshores and Ticino Mountains with town like Lucerne and Lugarno. Switzerland has the following factors that favor the development of tourism:

(1) *Good geographical location*: Switzerland is located at the centre of Europe; hence, it becomes the Centre of tourism industry to all European Countries.

(2) *Presence of beautiful scenery*: For example, the presence of Alps Mountains that are found in Alps ranges is the factor that attracts tourism in Switzerland. Plains also are the factor for tourism attraction.

(3) ***Presence of favorable climate:*** The general climate of Switzerland is cold snowy winters and warm sunny summer's sports such as skiing and ice skating as well as Swimming and Sunbathing acts as pulling factors.

(4) ***Presence of Good transport infrastructure:*** Like railways, Roads, harbors and Airports are the reason for development of tourism.

(5) ***Presence of Accommodation:*** Availability of accommodation like, Hotel, lodges, cottage camping site and guesthouse are the factors that influence tourism development in this country.

(6) ***Political stability in the country:*** Also, this factor support for the development of tourism in Switzerland.

(7) ***Hospitality:*** The Swiss people are hospitable and the personnel handling tourists are well trained and efficiency.

(8) ***The country is the Centre of international meeting:*** Many towns in Switzerland are used to host international convection like Geneva, Bern and Zurich. People attending these convections also take time off to tour the country.

Significance or Importance of Tourism in Switzerland:
1. Act as source of employment.
2. Source of foreign currencies
3. Improves international relations.
4. Source of Government Revenue.
5. Facilitate for the environmental conservation.
6. Facilitate the development of science and technology.

Problems Facing Tourism in Switzerland:
1. During winter there are heavy block movement on roads, railways and Runways.
2. Heavy competition from other countries like U.S.A is Switzerland facing.
3. Environmental pollution because some of tourists throw litter on the environment.

4. Faced with landslides, avalanches those are very dangerous to the tourists.
5. Tourism industry in Switzerland is faced with heavy competition from other sectors like manufacturing industry among others.

Case Study: Tourism in Namibia

Namibia is located in South Africa; its climate is desert because it is mostly covered by Namibia desert and Kalahari Desert. Major touristic attractions in Namibia include; The Cape cross, Seal reserve, and national parks. Factors favoring the development of tourism in Namibia are:

1. Improved infrastructures: This is the reason behind for tourism development in Namibia.

2. Strong tourism policy: Policy that encourage for the development of Tourism in Namibia.

3. Presence of touristic attraction: Like National parks, plateaus among others.

4. Great advertisement done by the government and private sectors: Is the way among others that support for development of tourism in Namibia.

5. Regional Co-operation: Namibia is the member of SADC hence through the Regional Tourism Organization of the Southern African Countries (RETOSA) Namibia is getting advantage for the growth of tourism.

Importance of Tourism in Namibia:
1. It is the source of revenue to the government.
2. Enable Namibia to improve social services.
3. Namibia somehow solved the problem of mass unemployment.
4. Facilitated for development of international relation.
5. Encouraged for the environmental protect in Namibia.
6. Ensured for the development of gross production(GDP) in the country
7. Namibia is earning more foreign currencies from tourism industry.

Problems or Challenges Facing Tourism Industry in Namibia
The following are the limitations that facing tourism in Namibia:

(1) High competition from agricultural sector; because the government of Namibia is over emphasizing on agricultural production.
(2) High competition in the market from other African countries; especially from South Africa and Botswana.
(3) Poor implementation of tourism policy. The government is none effectively implementing on the tourism policy.
(4) Lack of skilled personnel over tourism management.
(5) Poor investment in touristic sector industry. Government and Private sectors are not more investing in tourism like in other sectors.

Tourism Industry in Tanzania

Tanzania is the country that found in African continent, is among of the East Africa countries that involving in tourism industry. Tanzania is the one of the leading country in tourism attractions, which has a lot of National parks, National games and beautiful sceneries.

Tourism attraction in Tanzania are; National parks like Ngorongoro, Serengeti, Mikumi, and National games like Selous and beautiful sceneries like rivers, lakes, beaches, Mountains and forests.

Factors Favoring Tourism Development in Tanzania

Tanzania has different factors that favor for the development of tourism, some of them are:

1. *Peace and harmony.* Tanzania is the peaceful country that has no political instability. Tanzania has no civil war, religion war, tribe wars that may be seemed as the limiting factor for the tourists to come in Tanzania. This is the factor for tourism development in the country.

2. *Hospitality of the people of Tanzania.* Tanzanians have high degree of hospitality as well as the personnel that serving to the tourism industry have high degree of hospitality, hence this is the reason that makes for the development of tourism in the country.

3. *Government support.* The Tanzania government do support for the development of tourism in the country both through investment and advertisement.

4. *Presence of tourism attractions.* The presence of tourism attraction in the country in one way or another facilitates for the development of tourism industry in Tanzania. Tourism attractions are like National parks and games, Mountains, beaches, lake, River to mention by a few.

5. *Conducive climate.* Good climatic condition in the country, also in the factor for the development of tourism in Tanzania. Tanzania is found to the area of Tropic of Capricorn that favor for the tourism development.

6. *Availability of capital.* The availability of capital for the government to invest in tourism industry also is the reason for the development of tourism in the country.

7. *Presence of historical sites.* Presence of historical site like Bagamoyo ruins and Oldvai George and other archeological sites like Ismila in Iringa are examples that favor Tanzania to be the leading country in East African in tourism sector.

Problem Facing Tourism Industry in Tanzania

There are challenges that hinder tourism industry to be developed. The following are some of the problems that facing tourism industry in Tanzania:

1. Shortage of capital. Inadequate of capital to be invested in the tourism industry is the problem that challenging the sector of tourism in the country.

2. Poor transport and communication. The system of infrastructures and communication are not well improved hence lead to the challenges in the development of tourism in the country.

3. Poor marketing. This is due to the poor advertisement and promotion of Tanzanian tourism in the world's touristic market, hence Tanzania not much known on having many tourism attractions in the country.

4. *Poor tourism policies.* The policies of tourism in the country are not well developed and implement, hence said to be the problem on tourism development in the country.

5. *Crimes.* Presence of crimes around touristy areas is the problem that facing Tanzania in the sector of tourism. Crimes like robbery, theft and sometime attacks in the tourism camps are the challenging issues which discourage the coming of tourists in the country.

6. *Increase of population.* There is a high population around the tourism centers, which lead to the destruction of tourism attractions also is the challenge that facing tourism industry in Tanzania.

7. *Competition from other economic sectors.* Tourism industry in Tanzania is facing high competition from other sector like agriculture, mining, among others; hence many personnel are employed in such sectors, leaving the sector of tourism with no skilled labors.

8. *Competition from other countries.* Tanzania is facing competition from other country like Kenya, Uganda, and Congo mentioning by few, hence lead to the low number of tourists in the country.

Ways to be used in Increasing Income from Tourism Industry in Tanzania:
1. Marketing and publicity, through making advertisement
2. Promotion of domestic tourism by influencing internal tourism.
3. Expansion of tourism attractions.
4. Provision of tourism education to all stakeholders.
5. Presence of security by preventing crimes in tourism areas and camps.
6. Improvement of infrastructure and communication network.
7. Establishment of package tourism.

How to Promote Tourism in Tanzania?
1. There should be an improvement of transport and communication services.
2. There should be an improvement of accommodation network.
3. Improvement of both the domestic and international tourism marketing.
4. There should be well-trained personnel in Tourism sector.

5. There should be identification of new tourism attractions that are not known.
6. There should be protection of tourism attractions from destruction.
7. There should be well-developed policies of tourism industry that have to be implemented effectively.

TRIAL QUESTIONS

1. Define the following concepts:
   a) Tourism
   b) Eco-tourism (green tourism)
   c) Honey-pots
   d) Tourist

2. Mention the followings;
   a) Ten games reserves in Tanzania
   b) Ten nation games in Tanzania

3. Outline the factors that encourage the development of tourism in any country.

4. Tourism has grown fast now days, give three reasons in short.

5. What is the importance tourism in any country?

6. Show the negative effects of tourism in Tanzania.

7. Show the importance of eco-tourism to the local community in Tanzania.

8. Why should the local people be involved in tourism activities?

9. Outline the problems facing tourism in East Africa.

10. Identify the negative effects of population growth on the tourist industry.

11. How does tourism differ from other industries?

12. How can Tanzania improve its tourism industry?

13. "Tourism in Tanzania has a bright future. Why?

14. Draw a map of Tanzania to show the location of the game reserves and national parks.

15. Mention the tourism attraction (honey-port) in Tanzania.

16. How can the conflict in the nation park be solved?

17. (a) Name three tourism centers in:
     i.   Tanzania
    ii.   Switzerland
   iii.   Namibia
 (b) Draw a map of Tanzania and show some of the tourism attractions.

18. Explain five ways to address the negative impacts of tourism in Tanzania.

19. Briefly give any five factors that contribute to the growth and development of the tourism industry in Switzerland.

20. What problems are facing the tourism industry in Tanzania?

21. Suggest any five ways:
  a) To increase tourism income in Tanzania
  b) To promote tourism in Tanzania

CHAPTER 07:

SUSTAINABLE USE OF POWER AND ENERGY RESOUCES

Energy is the power required to carry out an activity. Power is the ability to do something (work). *Therefore,* Energy produces power that used to carry out an activity. Energy sources can be divided into two broad categories:
  (a)Renewable sources
  (b)Non-renewable sources

(a)Renewable Sources: Are those sources (resources) that cannot be finished or exhausted. For example, sun, wave, tides, geothermal steam and biogas or biomass. Renewable sources also are known as inexhaustible sources

(b) Non-Renewable Sources: These are sources that can be exhausted or finished. Nonrenewable sources, also known as exhaustible resources. Examples of Non Renewable resources are coal, petroleum, natural gas, fuel wood, nuclear energy and all radioactive mineral like uranium and plutonium.

Renewable Energy Sources and Non-Renewable Energy Sources:
1. Sun: The sun is the source of all the other sources of energy. This is because all the other sources of energy are in one way or another depends on the sun for their very existence. The Sun is the correction of hot gases. It produces solar energy, which is tapped in various ways by human and plants. Solar energy is used to produce chemical, heat and electric energy.

2. Waves and Tides: These are the strong movements of seawater. These movements are caused by the earth's rotation, the gravitational pull of the moon as well as the movement of water particles. Waves and tides can be tapped to produce mechanical power, which is in turn to generate electricity.

3. Wind: Differences in atmospheric pressure cause movement of air; this moving air is referred to as wind. Wind energy can be converted into mechanical energy that may then, in turn, be used to produce electricity.

4. Biomass (Biogas): This refers to the existing plant and animal life in the environment. Biomass produces several forms of power and energy. It may be tapped to produce heat energy, mechanical energy as well as light energy.

5. Coal: Coal is formed due to compression of vegetative matter over very long periods of time. Due to its being covered by layers of mud, the vegetative material did not decompose completely, turning into coal due to the pressure and heat from the earth's crust. It is black or brown in color. Coal it is used to produce heat energy. This heat energy may be used in different way including the generation of electricity.

6. Petroleum: Petroleum also referred to as crude oil. Oil is formed from fossilized remains of animals and plants. Used in producing mechanical energy, heat energy and light energy.

7. Natural Gas: Natural gas commonly occurs alongside petroleum. Like petroleum, it is formed due to the fossilized of plants and animals. Natural gas produces heat energy and light energy.

8. Uranium and Plutonium: These are two minerals, which are used to produce nuclear energy, that produce nuclear power. They occur naturally in the Earth's crust.

Sources and Types of Energy

The following is the table that shows sources and types of energy:

No.	Source Of Energy	Types Of Energy
01.	Sun	Solar, Mechanical, Electrical.
02.	Wave and tides	Electrical.
03.	Wind	Mechanical, Electrical.
04.	Biomass	Mechanical, (Biogas).
05.	Water	Mechanical, Electrical.

06.	Wood	Mechanical.
07.	Animals	Mechanical.
08.	Petroleum	Mechanical, Electrical.
09.	Natural gas	Mechanical.
10.	Coal	Mechanical, Electrical.
11.	Uranium	Nuclear or Atomic, Mechanical, Electrical

Methods Used in Extracting Energy and Power

The followings are the methods used to extract energy or power from their sources:

1. Coal: Coal is mined from the earth's crust in various countries in the world. These include China, USA, and South Africa. The energy from coal is tapped by burning the coal. This produces heart-energy, which is used in various ways. It can be used for domestic heating, in industrial furnace, or used to boil water and produce steam, that can be used to power machinery and produce electricity.

2. Petroleum: It is refined before it is used. It is mined from the depths of the earth's crusts and transported to refineries, where different products are obtained from it. The energy of petroleum and its products is also tapped mainly by burning. This burning produces heat energy, mechanical energy or light energy. Petroleum products may be used in industrial furnaces, to run machinery or produce light.

3. Natural Gas: Like petroleum, natural gas also requires to be refined before it can be used. This involves the separation of various gases. The energy is the natural gas that extracted through the burning of the gas. This produces heat energy, which is used for domestic heating, generating thermal electricity and industrial heating purposes.

4. Water: The energy in water may be tapped naturally or artificially. Naturally, waterfalls may be used to run turbines, which are used in the generation of electricity. Artificially, water may be channeled through pipes to high points from where it drops, turning turbines to generate electricity.

5. Biomass: This consists of plant and animal life. These are burned to give off heat energy as well as light energy. Plant residues, such as slashed grass or dry, dead leaves and processed agriculture waste such as Maize husks as well as lumbering residue such as saw dust; can also be burned to produce heat and light energy.

The heat energy may be used for domestic heating or used in industries in furnaces. Animal waste such as dried cow dung may be burned to produce heat energy. Combined with plant residue and light to decompose under controlled condition, it can be used in the production of biogas. This can be used for heating or lighting purposes.

6. Plutonium and Uranium: The energy in these two minerals is extracted through either of two processes. Nuclear fusion and nuclear fission involving the splitting of an atom stead to the release of large amount of heat that used to heat water and produce steam, which is in turn used to turn turbines that generate electricity.

7. Wind: The mechanical energy of wind is trapped in several ways. It may be used to turn windmills, which are used to generate electricity or to directly run machines such as grain grinding mills. It may be tapped by putting up sails to propel water vessel.

8. Geothermal Steam: The geothermal power in geothermal steam is extracted by directing it to run machines that produce electricity. Its heat energy can also be trapped by placing the materials to be heated over the hot steam.

Importance and Uses of Power and Energy Resources
The energy and power resources are important in the following ways:

1. Used in industry: Power and energy resources are used to produce energy and power to the industries. Power and energy are used to run machines, provide light, produce electricity and provide heat for processing goods.

2. Used for transportation: Motorcycles and vehicles, airplanes, trains and ships all need fuel to provide energy and power for them to work.

3. Important in Mining: Machines for mining and lighting inside and outside mines need power and energy.

4. Importance in Agriculture: Power and energy are used to run heavy farm machinery such as those used to plough or harvest crops. Most of these machines run on diesel, which is petroleum product.

5. Sources of Employment: Large numbers of people are employed in this sector both skilled and unskilled man power.

6. Sources of foreign exchange: The industry act as the source of foreign currency if energy and power resources are exported.

7. Sources of government revenue: Through taxes collected from this industry, the government tends to get revenue.

8. Improvement of transport and communication infrastructure: In the presence of power and energy resources in an area contribute to the improvement of transport and communication system because are needed so as to smooth the extraction of these resources.

9. Promotion of trade and other Industries: This human activity promote to the development of trade and other sectors because it integrate with other economic activities, like agriculture, transport system, and all social services which are in need to this human activity.

Problems or Challenges Facing Power and Energy Production
The following are the limitation facing power and energy production:

1. Change of climatic conditions: Occurrence of droughts and the general shortage in rainfall may lead to a fall in water level at waterfalls and dams at hydroelectric power stations. This leads to the reduction in power production.

2. Lack of varied energy resources in the country: Some countries have limited sources of energy, e.g. geothermal steam and uranium, hence countries depends on water and solar.

3. Poor technology: In most developing countries, there is lack technology for energy and power exploitation.

4. Lack of skilled labor: In some countries (developing countries) there also very few skilled people for setting up and operating equipment as well as conducting research in power and energy production methods, activities and technology.

5. High prices of some sources of energy: The price of petroleum on the world market, hence lead to the people to un-afford of buying it, since it is used also in the generation of thermal electricity.

6. Lack of capital: It is very expensive to set up energy and power generating facilities, hence some developing countries may not able to buy and meet these costs.

7. Environmental pollution: Energy and power production has been blamed for polluting the environment, hence this sector get high pressure to adopt methods that ensure little or no pollution of the environment.

8. Siltation: In generation of hydroelectricity may lead to the siltation in source of water. Siltation is the situation where silt (soil particle) accumulates in water reservoirs at hydroelectric power plants.

Ways to Address the Problem Facing Power and Energy Production
The following are the suggested ways in order to solve the problems facing power and energy production:

(1) Removal of silt to ensure that, the dam capacity is reduced by the accumulation of silt.

(2) Country should diversify their energy production to reduce the effect of such factors as petroleum prices and climate.

(3) Developing countries should ensure that, they keep up with technological advancement.

(4) Research should be carried out often to improve energy and power production method as well as to come up with new production methods as well as less environmental pollution.

(5) Establishment of colleges, universities and other higher learning institutions to train professionals in the energy and power production field.

(6) Countries should collaborate to raise adequate capital to fund the setting up of power and energy production.

Solar and Wind Power in the United State of America

The United States of America (USA) is the country that advanced in technology with a wealthy economy. It is a developed Country with great demand for power and energy for its industries and its large population.

Solar power accounts for a very small percentage of total energy production in the USA. It is mainly exploited in the sun areas of the country especially in California and Nevada. Wind power is more used compared to solar power in the USA. Wind power is used to generate 0.7% of the total electricity production in the country.

Wind power is used to run large farms, industries as well as generating electricity that is fed into the national grid. The wind power is tapped by the use of windmills. Texas is currently the largest wind power producer in the country followed by California. The wind power will generate about 1% of the total electricity produced in the country by the end of the year 2008.

The following are the Importance of Solar and Wind power in the USA:
(a) *Source of employment.* Solar and wind power sectors employ many Americans

(b) *Industrial development.* Industrial development depends on cheap and reliable availability of power and energy. Wind and solar energy continue to make this possible.

(c) *Agricultural development.* Wind power is used in large farms to provide electricity and heating. Also it is used in irrigating fields. This has promoted large-scale agriculture in the country.

(d) *Conservation of non-renewable energy.* Resources such as petroleum are ensuring that they do not run out too soon.

(e) *Reduced environmental pollution.* Solar and wind power do not pollute the environment as much as other resources such as petroleum.

(f) *Improved standards of living.* Solar and wind power have become an affordable sources of power for many Americans. Wind and solar power seemed to be cheap to many Americans; hence, this improved their standards of living.

The following are the problems facing solar and wind power in the USA:
(1)The cost of equipment used in tapping solar and wind power on large scale is quite high. This has led to the limited investment.

(2)The harnessing of solar and wind power is highly dependent on the prevailing weather conditions. In case there is little or no sunshine or low wind speed, then it is difficult to harness the power.

(3)People are still reluctant to change from the traditional energy sources such as hydropower.

Solutions to the problem facing solar and wind power in the U.S.A:
(1)Alternative source of the energy have been used to supplement solar and wind power.

(2)Associations and government departments have been formed to inform and educate people about the benefits of solar and wind power.

(3)Government supports as well as partnership have enabled the setting up of stations for wind and solar energy.

Hydroelectric power (H.E.P) and Biogas in Tanzania

1. Hydroelectric power

Hydroelectric power contributes the largest percentage of electricity generated in Tanzania. The Tanzania Electric supply company (TANESCO) is the main producer of HEP in Tanzania.

TANESCO produces electricity at several hydroelectric projects. The project include Nyumba ya Mungu and Hale on Pangani river, Lower Kihanji around the Kihanji and Mhalala water falls in the Udizungwa mountains in Southern highlands, Kidatu and Mtera on the Great Ruaha river and Stieglers Gorge on the Rufiji river. These projects have total installed capacity of generating 561 MW of electricity.

2. Biogas

As a way to reduce dependence on petroleum and other nonrenewable energy resources such as fuel wood, the Small Industries Development Organization (SIDO) introduced the use of biogas in Tanzania. Most of this biogas is produced for domestic use. There are over 700 biogas plants in Tanzania today. Most of these are located in rural areas where raw materials such as cow dungs are easily available.

Importance of HEP and Biogas production in Tanzania:

(1) *The use of Biogas has reduced environmental degradation.* In areas where it is available, people no longer need to cut down trees to get fuel wood. Biogas also does not emit fumes when it is burned.

(2) *Employment opportunity to Tanzanians.* Many people are employed to carry out the various activities involved in the generation of biogas and hydroelectric power.

(3) *Promotes development of other industries in the county.* Electricity in hydroelectric power stations has played an important role in the growth and growth of other industries in the county.

(4) *Improved standard of people's living in the rural areas.* The availability of biogas and HEP in rural areas has greatly improved the standards of living of the people. Those who have access to biogas no long have to speed many hours looking for wood and are therefore able to concentrate on other important activities.

Problems facing HEP and Biogas Production in Tanzania:

(1) *Unreliable climate condition.* Tanzania experience dry periods in summer season, hence this reduces hydroelectric power production leading to power rationing.

(2) *Lack of capital.* Tanzania is large country hence lack adequate capital to acquire and set up the Machinery and equipment needed to accommodate several electrical projects.

(3) *Siltation.* This reduces the volume of water in the dams. Thus, reducing capacity of electricity generation.

(4) *Lack of skilled personnel.* Setting up and operation of hydroelectricity power plants and biogas plants requires skilled personnel, but in Tanzania we lack such personnel hence this act as the sanction for HEP and biogas production in the country.

(5) *Reluctance by the people.* Some people are reluctant to adopt the Use of biogas. They consider it is dirty and lowly in status.

Solutions to the problems facing HEP and Biogas production in Tanzania:
   (a) Frequent dredging of reservoirs (removal of silt) to avoid siltation.
   (b) Development of other sources of power to reduce HEP which is highly affected by climate.
   (c) Establishment of training institutions to provide skilled personnel to work in power generation plants.

(d) Liberalization of power generation might lead to greater availability of funds for development of HEP and biogas production.

(e) Promotion and marketing by the government and other concerned organization will help to encourage people to adopt the production and Use biogas.

Lesson Tanzania Learns from the USA Energy and Power Production:
The following are some of the Lesson to be drawn by Tanzania from the USA energy and power production:

1. The government should support the development of various energy sources as USA does.

2. The government should form departments to encourage the development of alternative sources of energy such as solar power and wind power as USA do.

3. Diversity – Tanzania should diversify her energy sources to reduce the negative impacts of reduced production from one source.

TRIAL QUESTIONS

Qn1. Define the following terms:
a) Solar   (c) Energy   (e) Renewable source of power
b) Power   (d) Siltation   (f) Nonrenewable source of power

Qn2. With vivid example, differentiate between non-renewable and renewable sources of power.

Qn3. Describe the extraction of energy or power from any two sources of energy.

Qn4. (a) State five problems that faces HEP production in Tanzania
(b) Suggest solutions to the problem you have stated in above.

Qn5. Explain five reasons why energy or power resources are important

CHAPTER 08:

SUSTAINABLE MINING

Mining is the process of extracting minerals and fossil fuels from the earth's crust. Also mining is the process of extracting different minerals and fuels from the earth's ground. *Sustainable mining* refers to the controlled extraction of minerals and fossil fuels with minimum environmental destruction. Mining industry divided into two major types, namely:

(1) Metal mining industry.
(2) Non-metal mining industry.

1. Metal Mining Industry: This mining industry involves extraction of metal minerals like gold, copper and Iron among others.

2. Non-Metal Mining Industry: It is the type of mining industry that involves the extraction of nonmetals minerals like salt, oil, and diamond.

Types of Minerals
Types of minerals are in three main categories:

(1) Metallic minerals.
(2) Non-metallic minerals.
(3) Energy minerals.

1. Metallic minerals: these are types of mineral that comprises iron minerals. Examples of metallic minerals are gold, silver, led, and iron.

2. Non-metallic minerals: These are types of minerals that does not consist elements of iron. Examples of these minerals are asbestos and graphite.

3. Energy minerals: These are types of minerals that contain fossil materials. Examples of these minerals are coal, natural gas and petroleum.

Distribution of Mining Region in the World:
1. Coal: Coal is an organic mineral with a long history of usage by man. China is a leading producer of coal minerals in the world, followed by U.S.A,

European Union, South Africa. Tanzania also extracts coals for some extent at Mchuchuma.

2. *Petroleum:* Petroleum is the source of heat and lighting and used for lubricants of machines. Oil produces; diesel, kerosene and aviation fuel. The leading producers of petroleum are Saudi Arabia, Russia, United Arabs-Emirates, Nigeria and Angola. Tanzania is also in expectation for petroleum extraction.

3. *Iron Ore:* Iron ore processed to come up with iron, which is the most commonly used metal. Producers are China, Brazil, USA, Australia and South Africa.

4. *Diamond:* A diamond is hard types of stone, which is into various uses. Diamonds are used to cut glass, making rings bracelets and necklaces. Major world producers of diamond are South Africa (at Kimberley), Botswana, Russia and Australia. In Tanzania, diamond mined at Mwandui in Shinyanga region.

5. *Gold:* Gold is into various uses, especially in decoration, making rings bracelets and necklaces. Major world producers of gold are: South Africa, Ghana among others. In Tanzania, gold mined at Kahama, Geita and Nyamongo.

Methods of Mining
The following are the mains methods of mining:
  i.   Underground (shaft) mining method.
  ii. Open cast (strip) mining method.
  iii. Alluvial (placer) mining method.

I. Underground (shaft) Mining Method: It is the method, which is used to extract minerals that are found deep in the ground. The method involves digging a deep hole (shaft) to the lower level in the ground.

II. Open Cast Mining Method: It is the method that involves the removal of the upper surface layer of soil in which minerals are found. The method is cheap. In addition, this method it is known as *strip method.*

*III. Alluvial Mining Method***:** This is the method of mining that mainly used in extracting minerals in river valleys. This method is also known as *placer or panning method.*

Ways of Processing Various Minerals:

Mineral processing is the situation of converting mined minerals from actual kind into other kind ready for the intended use. The following are ways of processing various minerals:

*Copper processing***:** Copper mined as an ore. Copper crushed into small pieces, it is then mixed with water in additional with chemicals into a floatation machines. Copper particles floats and are the removed. These particles are dried and sent to the copper smelters. Smelters reduce the concentrates to copper blister. The copper blisters used to trace small pieces of gold, zinc or any other minerals.

Iron Processing: The process of iron involves crushing the ore to get small particles of the waste rock. The product then concentrated to form *pellets* which followed by production of *Pig iron* that made into steel by melting it to remove all of its impurities after which small amount of other metals are added make different types of steel. There are four (4) main forms of Iron ore:

(1) Hematite - This contains about 70% of Iron.
(2) Limonite – This contains less than 60% of Iron.
(3) Magnate – Whose iron contents is about 70%.
(4) Siderite – Which an iron contents is about 30%.

Gold Processing: The ore is crushed and dissolved in a solution of sodium cyanide. This chemical dissolves the gold particle leaving behind stone and other mineral waste. The sodium cyanide solution containing gold particle is drained off and mixed with Zinc dust, which causes the gold particles to solidify. The particles are then melted and molded into bars called *ingots*.

Contribution of the Mining Industry to the Development of Tanzania

Mining industry has the following economic importance in Tanzania:

1. Provide employment opportunities: The mining industry act as source of employment opportunities in the country because many people are employed in the sector, hence solve the problem of unemployment.

2. Led to the urbanization: Mining industry attracts many people to the area, hence led to the growth of towns; for example, at Mwandui, Greita and Kahama.

3. Facilitates to the development of other sectors: The mining industry facilitates to the development of other sectors like agriculture, trade, transportation and communication.

4. Provides of materials: Products from mining industry are the raw materials for the different uses to human activities. For example, salt for domestic uses, diamond for cutting glass and gypsum for cement making industry.

5. Act as the source of foreign currencies: Mining industry facilitates to the country in earning more foreign currencies that are uses for exportation by the government.

6. Mining industry contributes to the government revenue: Mining industry is the source of government revenue that can be used in different developmental activities in the country, like paying workers, provision of social services among others.

Effects of Mining Industry on the Environment
Mining industry has serious negative effects or impacts on the environment:

1. *Cause for the environmental pollution:* Ming activities cause for noise, air water and land pollution.

2. *Led to the soil erosion:* Mining activities may led to the loose of soil on the land that may be eroded easily.

3. *Cause for deforestation:* Mining involves cutting down trees, hence lead to the deforestation on the area. This leave the land bared with no vegetation cover.

4. *Lead to the land degradation:* Mining industry creates new features on the earth's surface, like large holes, hence land degradation.

5. *Cause for the loss of biodiversity.* Mining activities may lead to the death of organism and living things due to the disturbances of the environment.

Ways of Minimizing Effects of Mining Industry on the Environment
Some of the ways of minimizing the negative effects of mining industry on the environment are as follows:

(1) *Formulation of laws:* There should be created laws that may ensure for the protection of environment against the mining activities.

(2) *Provision of education:* All those who will engage in the extraction of minerals have to be given education on how to protect the environment.

(3) *Rehabilitation of land:* Once the minerals are exhausted, the lands should be rehabilitated through planting tree (both afforestation and reafforestation).

(4) *To carry extensive research:* Before an establishment of mining, there should be a research of the place so as to make the players to ensure the protection of environment.

(5) *Establishment of other economic activities*: There should be an establishment of other economic activities in order to avoid much engagement on mineral extraction that lead to the effect on the environment.

(6) *Prohibition in the use of bad method of mineral extractions that lead problems to the environment,* like that of open cast method of mining.

Oil Production in the Middle East
The Middle East is the largest oil-producing region in the world. The main producers of oil in the region are; Saud Arabia, Iraq, Kuwait, Iran, and the United Arabia-Emirate. Others are Qatar and Yemen. Most of these countries in the Middle East are the member of the *Organization of Petroleum Exploiting Countries (OPEC)* which plays the great roles of fixing the oil prices

Advantages or Importance of Oil Production in the Middle East:
(1) Source of employment opportunity.
(2) Source of foreign currencies.
(3) Promote to the improvement of social service.
(4) Facilitate to the improvement of transport and communication.
(5) Provision of energy and power.
(6) Promote international relation.
(7) Facilitates for the development of other economic sectors.

Activity:
Discuss for the factors influencing development of oil production in the countries of Middle East.

Production of Natural Gas in Tanzania

Natural gas is the products obtained from fossilized organic matter. Tanzania has managed to extract natural gas at Songosongo at Kilwa in Lindi region. The gas produced at Songosogo transported by pipeline to the destination. Also gas is produced in Mtwara region.

Advantages or Importance of Natural Gas in Tanzania:
(1) It is the source of employment opportunities in Tanzania.
(2) Provides power and energy for different use; both domestic and industrial uses.
(3) It is the source of government revenue.
(4) Led to the low cost of electricity.
(5) For some extent, it is environmental friendly.
(6) Can be easily transported and packaged for different uses.

Disadvantage of Natural Gas Production in Tanzania:
    a. Natural gas is high expensive.
    b. It is a non-renewable resource, hence can be exhausted.
    c. Need a lot of money for construction of pipeline.
    d. In construction of pipe line leads to the destruction of properties with a lot of compensation.

TRIAL QUESTIONS

1. Define the following terms:
   a. Mining.
   b. Mineral.
   c. Sustainable mining.
   d. Mineral processing.

2. Write short notes on the following:
   a) Mining industry.
   b) Types of mining methods.
   c) Types of minerals.
   d) Minerals processing.

3. Explain for the factors that influences for the development of mining industry.

4. Highlight for the general economic importance of mining industry.

5. What are the general negative effects of mining industry?

6. Discuss for the effects of mining on the environment.

7. Suggest for the possible solutions of negative effects of mining industry.

8. Shows the role of mining industry in the economic development in Tanzania.

9. Identify the factors limiting mining development in Tanzania.

CHAPTER 09:

TRANSPORT

By definition, transport is the movement of goods and people from one place to another. There are three common types of transport.
   a) Air transport.
   b) Water transport.
   c) Land transport.

Land Transport

This involves the movement of goods and people on land surface. The major means of transport on land include:
   i.   Human transport (human portage)
   ii.   Animal transport.
   iii. Road transport.
   iv.   Railway transport.
   v.   Pipeline transport.

Human transport

Human transport is where people carry light goods from one place to another. Human transport is the oldest form of transport in the world. People they carry goods on their heads, backs, shoulder, or hold them in their hands.

Sometimes they can use wheelbarrow, handcarts or trolleys for easy movement. Human transport is common where other forms of transport cannot be used e.g. crowded areas. The following are the advantages of human transport:

1. Available whenever it is needed. It may be available in areas where other form of transport cannot be used.

2. It is very cheap. It is very affordable means of transport that can be used everywhere.

3. It is safety. It is safe than road, air, or water transport, because few accident occur during transportation.

4. It is flexible. Human transport can be used to transport goods to various places in and in towns and rural areas.

5. *It complements with other means of transport.* It complement with road and rail when goods arrive at a destination they have to be moved by people to the destination.

6. *Does not pollute environment.* It causes little or no noise, no smoke and no oil spills unlike other forms of transport.

The Following are the Disadvantages of Human Transport:
1. It is slow and tedious.
2. Cannot be used to carry heavy or bulk goods.
3. Depends on human strong and healthy.
4. It is only suitable for short distance.

Animal Transport

Animal transport is the means of transport mostly used in areas where other forms of transport can be used alongside human transport (e.g. in deserts and mountainous areas). The animals used include camels, horses, elephants, donkey, and cows among.

Animals that carry goods on their backs are referred to as *pack animals* whereas those that pull carts are referred to as *draught animals*. The following are the advantages of animal transport over human transport:

(i)   It is faster than human transport.
(ii)   It can be used to carry heavier goods over long distances
(iii)   It can be used in places with conditions e.g. in desert areas

Road Transport

Road transport involves the use of various types of vehicles, motorcycle and bicycle. There are weather and dry weather. Motorable tracks are small feeder roads used by people in vehicles and on motorcycles and bicycle during the dry season. The following are advantages of road transport:

(1) Many vehicles can be used.

(2) Road transport is quite flexible, because it connects many places and can be used at varying.

(3) It is faster than human transport and animal transport.

(4) Construction and maintenance of roads is relatively cheaper than that of railway.

(5) Road transport complements other means of transport like air, railway or water transport.

The following are Disadvantages of Road transport:

(1) Road transport is easily affected by weather conditions, for example during heavy rain.

(2) Have more instances of accidents.

(3) Vehicles and motorcycles invite gases that pollute the environment (especially air).

(4) Road transport suffers with congestion problems hence causes for delay and consumes a lot of time.

(5) Needs frequent maintenance.

Railway transport

This is the transport that involves moving good and people from one place to other using trains on rails. The following are advantages of railway transport:

(1) It is relatively cheaper than road transport.

(2) Carry both heavy and bulky good as well as many passengers.

(3) There is low effect of weather condition on railway transport.

(4) Recantation and maintenance not frequent as road

(5) Have little accident unlike to road transport.

(6) Not affected by congestion as it the ease with road transport.

(7) Modem passenger trains (called bullet trains) are very fast and efficient.

Below are the Disadvantages of Railway transports:

(1) Railway constriction is expensive and takes a long period of time unlike road construction.

(2) Railway transport depend other means of transport, like road, human and animal transport to move cargo into the railway starts.

(3) Most of railway transport is low (except of bullet trains).

(4) Railway transport is not economical for transporting goods and people over short distances, and not economical for transport few or light goods.

(5) Railway transport is not flexible.

(6) They have few stations to serve the areas.

Pipeline transport

Pipeline transport involves the movement of fluids or liquid and gases from one place to another through pipes. Such liquid and gases include; oil, water, sewage and natural gas. Pipes are made of steel or plastic tubes with an inner diameter of between 10cm and 120cm connected to each other

"Multi- product pipeline" is the pipeline that transports two or more products in the same pipeline. Examples of pipeline are the Tanzania, Zambia Mafuta (TAZAMA) pipeline. The following are Advantages of pipeline transport:

(1) Does not pollute the environment.

(2) No or low accident.

(3) Fast means of transport (No congestion).

(4) Not affected by weather.

(5) Can be laid on land, underground or underwater, making pipeline transport flexible.

(6) Although the initial development of pipeline is expensive, the operation and maintenance costs are low.

(7) It complements other transport system.

Disadvantages of Pipeline Transport:

(1) Pipelines are expensive to develop.

(2) Pipeline can only transport fluid and gases only.

(3) Leakage can occur if there is no clear supervision and maintenance.

(4) It is not good for rare or occasional use.

(5) Depends from other means of transport.

Air Transport

This is the movement of goods and people from one place to another through air. It involves the use of aircraft, such as airplanes, helicopter and hot air balloons. There are two types of air transport, which are; *domestic* and *international* transport. The following are advantages of air transport:

(1) It is faster and suitable in the transport of goods that are perishable and sick people and animals.

(2) Air transport is not affected by physical barriers like mountains, rivers and lakes.

(3) Air transport is conformable in traveling for long distances.

(4) Air transport is good in time management.

(5) Air transport is flexible as routes and planes can be changed when the need arises.

(6) Air transport is convenient for the transportation of delicate as well as valuable goods because of its high level of security and safety.

Below is Some of Disadvantages of Air Transport:

(1) Air transport is heavily affected by weather.

(2) Air transport is very expensive.

(3) In case of accidents, a lot damage and loss are experienced.

(4) Need high trained personnel to work in air transport.

(5) It is not suitable for transporting bulky goods over long distance.

(6) It is only available to the places that have airports (exceptional helicopters).

(7) It is highly dependent on other forms of transport.

(8) It faced with security problems because it faced with hijackings and terrorist attack.

Water Transport

This is the movement of goods and people from one place to another over water using water vessels such as boats, ships to mention by few. There are two categories of water transports as namely: *Inland water transport* which involve the movement of people and goods over inland water bodies such as rivers, lakes and canals and *Sea or ocean transport* which involves the movement of people and goods over the oceans and seas.

Advantages of water transport:

(1) It is most suitable means for transporting heavy and bulky goods over long distances.

(2) Minimal construction costs are incurred in this means of transport.

(3) There is minimal congestion in water transport.

(4) Some cargo ships are especially designed to transport certain specific types of cargo e.g. petroleum or oil, food stuffs, or animals.

(5) Involves minimal cost for transportation of goods and people.

Disadvantages of water transport:

(1) Water transport is one of the slowest means of transport.

(2) Modern shipping vessels are expensive and port construction as well.

(3) Water transport is greatly affected by changes in climatic conditions, especially in navigable rivers and lakes.

(4) Water transport is limited to areas adjacent to water bodies.

(5) It depends from other means of transports.

Patterns of Major Transport System in East Africa

Transport systems in East Africa mainly connect urban centers, and coastal centers that are productive areas. For example, the railway lines in Kenya, Uganda and Tanzania connect urban centers as well as other productive areas to the coast.

Indeed railways were built to connect the rich interior of Kenya, Uganda and Tanzania. Main roads also connect urban centers to rural areas through several feeder roads that are connected to these main roads. Railways and roads connect to or pass close to airports, seaports and inland ports, this because roads and railways are highly complement (with) water and air transport.

Importance of Transport Industry in East Africa

A good transport system is important for the social and economic development of a country. Below is an outline of some of the reasons about why transport is important:

(1) Promotes unity and understanding. Transport system contributes significantly to unity and understanding due to the people to travel from one place to another and by interacting with others.

(2) Encourages development of other industries. Transport network encourages the development of other industries, such as tourism, Agriculture and manufacturing.

(3) Enable easy movement of people and goods from one place to another.

(4) Influence development of settlements. Settlements are more likely to develop where there is easy access to transport routes and facilities.

(5) Transport network facilitate in exploitation of natural resources in different areas then to be transported from one place to another.

(6) Act as source of employment and enhancement (facilitation) of trade

Problems Facing Transport Industry in East Africa

Transport industry in these countries of East Africa faced with several problems, including the following:

(1) Political problems. The three East African countries have been at peace for a considerable period of time but these countries failed to invest much on improving transport network.

(2) Railways in East African countries have different sizes of gauge, hence make impossible for connectivity of three countries through railway lines.

(3) Presence of mountainous and rugged terrain in some parts of East African countries makes very expensive to build roads, railways or air ports.

(4) Presence of thick vegetation in East African states makes difficulties in construction of road and railways.

(5) Most of navigable rivers and lakes are seasonal (temporally) where as heavy rain and drought limit river navigability.

(6) Landlocked countries like Uganda do not have access to the sea or ocean.

(9) Frequently attacks of mass movement (landslides and mudflow), soil erosion and floods.

(10)   Lack of capital; lack of skilled labor and high cost of fuel is the challenging problem.

Measures to Address the Problems of Transport Industry in Tanzania

The following are some of the measures in which can be taken in order to alleviate the problems of transport industry in Tanzania:

(1) Development of manpower or workforce for the various fields of transport and communication through establishment of specific courses targeting these areas.

(2) The country should closely consult in developing their transport infrastructure to ensure connectivity in all places.

(3) Formulation of policies and laws that promote the growth of transport industry.

(4) The government should increase its oil reserves so that to avoid negative effects of fluctuating oil prices.

(5) Intensified revenue collection as well as seeking financial assistance from the developed countries in order to obtain capital for the development of the transport infrastructure in the country.

TRIAL QUESTIONS

Qn1. Define the following terms:
a) Transport
b) Air transport
c) Animal transport
d) Water transport
e) Road transport
f) Railway line
g) Pipeline transport
h) Human transport

Qn2. Write short notes on the following terms:
a) Transport.
b) Air transport.
c) Animal transport.

d) Water transport.
e) Road transport.
f) Railway line.
g) Pipeline transport.
h) Human transport.

Qn3. (i) Name the main types of transport in the world.

(ii) Write five advantages of the types of transport and five disadvantages of these types of   transport.

Qn4. (a) Describe the patterns of transport in East Africa.

(b) Explain the importance of transport in East Africa.

Qn5. What are the problems limiting the development of the transport industry in East Africa?

Qn6. Suggest any three ways to address the problems facing Tanzanian transport industry.

CHAPTER 10:

SAMPLE QUESTIONS

1. "Hydro-electric power (HEP) supply in Tanzania is a problem". What are the causes?

2. Explain the problems facing mining industry in Tanzania.

3. "Human activities may result in desertification". Give suggestions on how to solve the problems of desertification.

4. Describe the importance of tourism in our economic development.

5. "Economic development in Tanzania and other countries depends much on transport" Briefly explain.

6. "The use of fuel wood as a source of energy among Tanzanians will continue for many years to come". By giving five points, briefly explain why.

7. "Wind power is renewable and free from pollution through it has some problems". Explain five problems facing production of wind power.

8. Suggest five ways of improving the hydroelectric power supply in Tanzania.

9. With six points show how a long distance to and from water sources can affects girls.

10. Briefly discuss five points on the importance of manufacturing industries to the world economy.

11. Describe the advantages of natural gas from Songosongo to our economy.

12. Forests play great roles in human life. Do you agree? Why?

13. Suggest ways of improving tourism industry in Tanzania.

14. What are the problems facing timber industry in the Congo basin?

15. Describe the problems facing agriculture in Tanzania.

16. Geographers prefer watching weather forecasting news every day. Do they benefit by watching such news? (Give five reasons for your answer).

17. Briefly discuss the importance of pastoralism in East Africa.

18. Water plays great roles in sustaining life in our planet Earth. Do you agree? Why?

19. Why most of African rivers are not fully utilized for navigation?

20. Describe necessary conditions for establishing hydroelectric power (HEP).

21. Analyze how livestock can be improved in Tanzania.

22. Explain the benefits brought by agricultural sector in Tanzania.

23. Explain the negative impacts of tourism in East Africa.

24. What are the ways of improving small-scale agriculture?

25. What are the problems facing marine transport in Africa?

26. Explain how Tanzania is going to benefit from natural gas.

27. Briefly explain the problems facing the harnessing of hydroelectric power (HEP) in East Africa.

28. Describe the advantages and disadvantages of small-scale agriculture.

29. Explain basic characteristics of nomadic pastoralism.

30. What is the economic importance of water?

31. Suggest ways of improving tourism industry in Tanzania.

32. Describe six problems associated with exploitation of forest resources.

33. Explain factors influencing the location of any industry in the developing countries like Tanzania.

34. How do you think Tanzania benefits from having hydroelectric power station? Give out six points.

35. Discuss on the effects of population growth on the tourism industry.

36. Outline at least five ways of reducing pollution in developing nations like Tanzania.

37. Discuss the disadvantages of deforestation in your country.

38. Show eight importance of transportation in the development of the country.

39. Give suggestion on how to solve the problems of desertification.

40. Write the important conditions for developing tourism in Tanzania.

41. Explain for measures should Tanzania undertake to improve industrial development.

42. Describe the problem facing power and energy production.

43. Analyze the impact of the mining industry on the environment.

44. Justify the problems facing livestock keeping in Tanzania.

45. Explain the ways that can be used to conserve water resources in the country.

PART TWO

HUMAN GEOGRAPHY

CHAPTER 11:

CONCEPTIALIZATION TO HUMAN POPULATION

A population study is also termed as population analysis or population substantive. Population studies deals with the relationship between demographic variables and non-demographic variables. Demographic variables include fertility, mortality and age at first birth and age at first marriage. Non-demographic variables include income, education, religion and occupation.

Substantive demographers are mostly social scientists, especially sociologists, economists and geographers who are interested in effect of the non-demographic variables on the basis of available data e.g. how change in education can affect fertility or mortality.

All related to population studies are mathematical demography, formal demography or technical demography; it deals with methods, techniques in which are used to study the mechanism of population change. Mathematical demography is the study of human population and analysis through mathematical models and deals with demographical variables in a mathematical way. Technical demographers are usually mathematicians or staticians.

Current issues which are concerned with population studies are gender issues, current issues on population, population policies, population and environment. The world population is increasing ever more rapidly. This is because it increases in geometrical fashion (i.e. 2, 4, 8, 16, 32, 64, 128…) rather than arithmetically (i.e. 1, 2, 3, 4, 5,). Death rate and infant mortality rates have been drastically reduced so that more children grow up and themselves have families.

Therefore; enormous as the world population is mere numbers do not present problem if all the people in area can be fed, clothed, educated, and employed. But this cannot always be done and this is why population growth creates problems.

Sometimes the main difficulties arise because people are not distributed evenly over the earth and because the age and sex structure of population varies widely from country to country. Only in term of these factors can we discuss whether a country is under-or- over-population.

Thomas Malthus was an English clergy who in 1798, published an essay on the principle of population in which he put forward the view that, "the power of population is indefinitely greater than the power of the earth to produce substance for man!" He thought that a balance could only be maintained if famine, diseases, or war periodically increased the death rate and reduce the population growth. His pessimistic ideas were accepted by several others nineteenth century scholars in England and France.

Definition of Terms:

(a) *Population* refers to all number of people who inhabit an area, region or country or continent.

(b) *Human population* is the total number of people occupying a particular area at a particular time.

(c) *Demography* is the scientific study of human population.

(d) *Development* is the situation whereby a person increases in different skills and material wealth. Development is said to take place when poverty is reduced among the large number of people

(e) *Population size* is the total number of people inhabiting a specific area over a specified period of time.

(f) *Population density* refers to the relationship between *total numbers of population* in an area with the total area occupied by population in kilometer square.

(g) *Population structure* refers to how population is made up in term of composition of population of sex, age, occupation, income, education, and other attributes.

(h) *Population explosion* is the suddenly growth of population related to resources and food or accommodation availability.

(i) *Zero population* is referred as grow or decline of population. Also zero population sometimes can be defined as stationary population growth.

(j) **Dependency ratio** is the ratio between people engaged in production and those unproductive ones.

(k) **Sex** refers to the natural biological differences between men and women.

(l) **Gender** refers to the social or cultural distinction associated with being male or female. Man; indicate boy, male sex and masculine social role while women; indicates girl, female sex, and feminine social role.

(m) **Gross Domestic Product (D.G.P)** is the total market value of all final goods and service produced with the domestic territory (country) in a year.

(n) **Brain drain** is the migration or movement of large numbers of educated and very skilled people from their own country to another country where they tend to live and work due to better conditions and payment.

(o) **Population parameter** is the true value of a population attribute.

(p) **Sample statistic** is an estimate, based on sample data, of a population parameter.

Characteristics of Population:

Human population is characterized by the following characteristics:

1. *Population has age and sex structure.* Any population has the composition/proposition of age and sex.

2. *Population characterized by variation in the level of development and technology.*

3. *Population is unevenly distributed over the area.* Some areas have low population and other area have high population hence no equal distribution of population from one place to another.

4. *Population is dynamic.* Population is dynamic because due to migration, birth and death and not static or stagnant or station because there is an increase or decrease of population.

5. *Population usually faced with problems*. Population is faced with problems like decease (HIV/AIDs), environmental calamities (famine, floods, earth, quakes among others).

Importance of Studying Population (*Why do we study population?*):
1. It helps us to understand the distribution of people in a particular area, region or country.
2. It helps geographers to know the total numbers of the population of an area.
3. It may help the government to provide the social service of the known number of population in the country.
4. Helps to understand age and sex structure of a particular population in relations to number of population.
5. Facilitates in knowing social dependency and working group in the country.

Population and Sustainable Development

Sustainable development is a process through which people can satisfy their needs and improve their quality of life in the present but not compromise the ability of future generations to meet their own needs. *Population sustainability* means that, the population does not use more ecological resources than nature can regenerate.

Population can be unsustainable due to:
1. Rapid population growth
2. Overconsumption to the available resources
3. Loss of biodiversity
4. Shortage of resource
5. Environmental pollution and degradation

For most people, aspiring to a better quality of life means improving their standards of living as measured by income level and use of resources and technology. However, sustainable development also requires equity. For example, economic and environmental goals will not be sustainable unless social goals – such as universal access to education, health care and economic opportunity – are also achieved.

At any level of development, human impact (I) on the environment is a function of population size (P), per capita consumption (C) and the environmental damage caused by the technology (T) used to produce what is consumed. This relationship is often described as a formula:

$$I = P \times C \times T$$

Currently, people living in the North have the greatest impact on the global environment. However, as standards of living rise in the South, the environmental consequences of population growth will increase. Ever-increasing numbers of people aspiring, justifiably, to 'live better', also increases the potential for damage to the environment beyond what we are already witnessing.

The debate over the environmental challenges of population growth cannot be reduced to assigning blame. Patterns of consumption and resource use in the industrialized countries of the North are certainly responsible for much environmental degradation in both the North and South. However, growing populations, whatever their levels of consumption, also place a burden on resources and the environment. Both current and new consumers need to address the consequences of their level

Relationship between population and development:
1. Population provides labor supply in all productive activities.
2. Population provides markets for market products.
3. Population act as the sources in development of science and technology.
4. Population is the means in solving population problems in social and economic development.

Indicators for economic development:
1. G.D.P per capital (high or low).
2. Literate rate (high or low).
3. Poverty rate (high or low).
4. Life expectancy (high or low).
5. Percentage of people employed in agricultural sector (high or low).
6. Vehicle ownership (per 1, 000 people).
7. Diseases (high or low depending to the type of diseases)

CHAPTER 12:

POPULATION DISTRIBUTION AND CHANGE

POPULATION DISTRIBUTION

The world distribution of population in term of continents and countries, the world's population is very ill-balanced. More than half of the world's people live in Asia (excluding the former USSR) which accounts for only one-fifth of the world's land area, while north, central and south America together, occupy more than a quarter of the land surface, have only one-seventh of population the African continent also accounts for a quarter of land surface but has just over one-tenth of world population.

On the other hand, Europe, whose area is only one twenty-fifth of the total, has about one-ninth of the world's population. The inhabited area of the world's land surface is called *"ecumen"* and uninhabited or sparsely populated areas are referred to as *"non-ecumen"*.

Definition Population Distribution

Definitions of population distribution are based on comparison. Population distribution is the way in which people are spread over the space or an area. Population distribution can also be defined as is the occurrence or non-occurrence of people in a certain area. Population distribution is either low number of people or high number of people in an area.

Therefore; Population distribution varies from one place to another hence population is unevenly distributed. In one way or another, population distribution may be similar with or goes with population density. By definition, population density is the number of people and the area they occupy, or sometimes referred to the number of people per unit area. Population density distinguished by high density (densely populated) to low density (sparsely populated).

Factors Influencing Population Distribution (and Population Density)

Population distribution and density are influenced by physical factors, human factors, historical factors, political factors, and economic factors.

(a) *Physical Factors /Natural Factors*

1. Climate:

In this factor, rainfall and temperature are the main elements of climate. Areas with reliable rainfalls do attract high population, but where there is poor rainfall like in desert areas, there is low population. In addition, area with very high (harsh) temperature do not attract many people, while the areas with low (moderate) temperature, attracts many people.

2. Relief (topography):

Where the slope is steep, there is low population due to the poor soil and nature of the land. But, where there are gentle, slopes or flat surface, there is high population since the soils are good. Sometimes highland areas do attract people due to the good climatic condition or people being free from floods unlike to the low land areas.

3. Vegetation:

The area that is densely vegetated, people are discouraged to live in such areas due to the presence of harsh wild animals and poor transport and communication system unlike to the areas that are sparsely vegetated (there are many people).

4. Soil (edaphic factor):

Infertile soil discourage settlement since does not support agriculture. While good and fertile soil attracts many people, good example is the place of river Nile in Egypt, and Southern parts of Kilimanjaro Mountain.

5. Mineral and energy resources:

The areas with minerals and energy resources attract population (for example in Geita and Kahama in Tanzania). Unlike to the places that have no minerals and energy sources, the population of such areas tends to be very low.

6. Natural calamities:

Areas faced with natural hazards like flood, earthquakes, Tsunami, drought; therefore, areas having these catastrophes does not influence people to live in such areas; hence there must be low population in the area. While in the areas with absence of frequent attacks of natural catastrophes, normally the areas tend to be populated.

7. Biological factor (disease and pests):
People like settling in areas which are free of diseases and pests, while the place that are frequently attacked by diseases (e.g. malaria, HIV/AIDS, Tb, Ebola) and pests like locus people do not prefer to get settled on such areas hence the areas will be low populated.

(b) *Human Factors*
These factors also known as anthropogenic factors which are those including the following factors:

1. Political factors:
Area with political stability, peace and harmony tend to attract people and mostly such areas are more populated, while areas or places with political instability like presence of civil wars, tribe wars, ethnic wars and region wars tend to discourage people to settle in such areas. In addition, government policies that influence resettlement scheme, creation of National parks and forest reserves also influence population to be low on such areas.

2. Social cultural aspects:
Traditional beliefs like superstation influence low population to the area, while in absence of such beliefs, population seemed to be high in an area. Some tribes do not leave the areas because their ancestors used to live on such place hence high population may be found in such areas.

3. Economic factors:
Present of employment opportunities, banks, markets and industries influence the places to be highly populated unlike to the place that has no such influences hence there might be low population.

4. Transport and communication:
In presence of transport and communication in places may also influence high population density unlike to the places that have not transport and communication system. Transport and communication influence marketing, social services, security and accessibility therefore act as the pull factor for high population in any place.

5. Historical factors:

Low population in some place of Africa influenced by the effects of slave trade and colonization by Europeans also influence the variation of population as well as tribal conflicts and wars hence variation in population distribution. There some areas were favored by colonial masters through being given infrastructures and social services in which caused uneven distribution of population up to then.

POPULATION CHANGE

Population change refers to the increase and decrease of population in a particular area at a given time. Population change is the result of change in birth, death and migration. _Population change also can be determined as *population dynamics*. Sometimes population change or growth can be described by the increase of population (is the positive population growth) and the decrease of population (is the negative population growth).

Population change can be:
1. Change in size.
2. Change in structure.
3. Change in distribution.
4. Change in composition.

Components of Population Chance

Components of population change (population dynamics) involve the following:
  (i)   Fertility or Birth
  (ii)   Death or Mortality
  (iii) Migration (both emigration and immigration)

<u>*Note*</u> (1) Birth and Death are the natural change while migration is the Artificial Change.

(2) Population change has input, output and process (see the model provided on the following page):

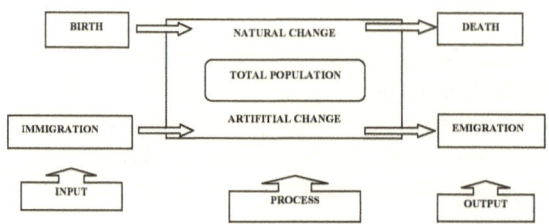

Birth Rate or Fertility Rate

Fertility rate refers to the occurrence of live birth in a population. *Fertility* refers to the ability to conceive or to reproduce.

$$Fertility\ rate = \frac{\underline{Live\ Birth}}{Population} \quad x\ 1000$$

Birth rate is measured by crude Birth rate, which is calculated as follows

$$C.\ B.\ R = \frac{\underline{No\ of\ live\ Birth}}{Total\ population} \quad x\ 1000$$

It is called crude birth rate, because it includes all ages and both sexes. *Live birth* is ability of women to bear a child. Live birth or still birth is called *fecundity*. Lack of fecundity is called infecundity or sterility. Infecundity is the inability of a woman to bear a child especially for those who cannot give a live birth.

Why High Fertility Rate?

The following are some of the reasons for the high fertility rate:
- (i) Improved health measures and medical services.
- (ii) Younger age marriage (early marriage)
- (iii) Cultural factors like having many children are the source man power, prestige and security. High birth rate is due to naming relatives, sex preferences and poor family palming.

Mortality or Death Rate

Mortality or death rate refers to the number of deaths within the population. *Infant mortality rate* is the number of deaths in a first year of live per 1, 000 live births. *Child mortality rate* is the number of deaths of children aged between 1 and 5 year per 1, 000 births. *Adult mortality rate* refers to the number of adult dying per 1, 000 of the total population. Mortality measured in term of Crude Death Rate (CDR).

Why High Death Rate?

Reasons for high death Rate are due to:

(i) Poor social services in medical and health services.
(ii) Diseases.
(iii) Wars.
(iv) Accidents.
(v) Poverty.

Factors Influencing Population Change

The following are the factors that may influence the increase or decrease of population:

1. Birth rate. High fertility rate may lead to the increase of population (look for factors that cause high birth rate).

2. Death rate. Mortality rate may cause for the decrease of population. (Refers to the causes of death rate).

3. Migration. Migration refers to the movement of people from one place to another at a given period of time with specific reasons. Migration can be categorized into two; *Emigration* and *Immigration*. Migration may also influence for the population change through both the increase (immigration) and decrease (emigration) of population to a particular area

4. Cultural Beliefs. Cultural beliefs may lead to the increase of population through; early marriage, sexual preferences, naming relatives etc.

5. Health services. Poor Health services may cause for the increase of death hence population change. While, if there are improved social services like hospital may lead to the increases of birth lives hence population increase may occur.

Effects of Population change

The effects of population change are into effect on the individual levels and effect on the national levels.

Effect of Population Change at Individual Level

Fertility rate results in a large number of children that family has to look after. Very many children may cause poor health of the mother. High impact mortality rate in a family may lead to family problem like witchcraft for blaming relatives or neighbors that they caused for mortality of the impacts.

Migration has the following impacts at individual levels:

(1) *Separation of spouses*. Due to the one have migrated to other place away with his or her spouse.

(2) *Spread of disease*. One person may cause for spread of disease in the fact that a migrant from a particular area may spread certain decease to his or her destination area. Such decease is like HIV/AIDs, Tb and cholera are easily to be spread.

(3) *Cultural destruction*. Due to the people may interact with other traditions, may lead to the alteration of culture of a person.

Effect of Population Change at National Level

It is very common to the industrialized countries. Decrease of Death rate may lead to the increase of population in the country hence over population in the country that may cause for unemployment, high pressure on resources and services. But in least developing countries, death rate is high that may lead to the effect of low population in the countries that may lead to the shortage of man power, underutilization of resources among others.

Measurements of Population Change and Balancing Equation

The following is the balancing equation for population change (population components):

$$Pt - Po = (B - D) \pm (I - O)$$

Mathematically

Births – Deaths = Natural Increase (NI)
In-migration – Out-migration = Net Migration (NM)

Therefore; NI + NM = Population Change

$$Pt - Po = (B\text{-}D) + (I\text{-}O) = NI + NM$$
$$Thus,\ Pt = Po + (B\text{-}D) + (I\text{-}O)$$

Where:
Pt = Population at the end
Po = Population at the beginning
B = Birth between 2 periods
D = Death between 2 periods
O = Out-migration
I = In-migration

Worked example: Population change between 1999 and 2000. Population of 1st January 1999 = 20, 333 people. During 1999 births were 500, deaths were 250, in-migration were 123 and out-migration were 32. What is the population on 1st January 2000.

Solution
The formula is: $Pt - Po = (B - D) \pm (I - O)$
Pt = ??, Po = 20, 333, B = 500, D = 250, I = 123 and O = 32.

$$Pt - 20,\ 333 = (500 - 250) \pm (123 - 32)$$
$$Pt = 20,333 + (500 - 250) + (123 - 32)$$
$$= 20,\ 333 + 250 + 91$$
$$Pt = 20,\ 674$$
There; population change is 20, 674 – 20, 333 = 341 people.

Population Growth Rate
Rate of population adjusted for birth, death and migration. Rate is expressed as **'r'** indicating percentage (%) growth per annum. Rate can be positive (+) or negative (-) i.e. increase or decrease. Population growth rates are established by models based on demographic statistic. There are two (2) models population growth rate namely:

1. *Geometric growth rate model:* calculated by the following formula:

$$r = \sqrt[n]{\frac{Pt}{Po}} - 1$$

2. *Exponential growth rate model:* calculated by the following formula:

$$r = \frac{1}{n}log\ e\left(\frac{Pt}{PO}\right)$$

Whereby: *Pt = population at the end*
Po = initial population
n = interval between counts (Pt – Po in years)
e = base of natural logarithm (e = 2.72).
r = is growth rate

Qn: Population of Tanzania in 1988 was 23,174,336; in 2002 the population was 34,584,607. Estimate the growth rate using the two models.

Solution

(a) Geometric Growth rate:

$$n = 2002 - 1988 = 14\ years$$

$$r = \sqrt[14]{\frac{34584607}{23174336}} - 1$$

$$r = \sqrt[14]{1.492366685} - 1$$

$$r = 1.029010205 - 1$$

r = 0.029010205

As percentage; r = 0.029010205 x 100%

r = 2.9% per annum

(b) Exponential Growth rate:

$$r = \frac{1}{14}log\ e\left(\frac{34584607}{23174336}\right)$$

Note: '*log e*' = '*ln*' which is 2.72

Therefore; $r = \frac{1}{14}$ *ln* (1.492366685)

$$\frac{ln}{14} \ (1.492366685)$$

$$\frac{2.72 \ x \ 1.492366685}{14}$$

$$r = \frac{4.059237383}{14} = 0.28597374$$

As Percentage, r = 0.28597374 x 100% = 29% (approximated)
OR
As Percentage, r = 0.028597374 x 100% = 2.9% (approximated)

Assignment1 (Interpolation): The annual rate of increase in Chile between 1960 and 1970 was estimated at 2.4 percent. What was the population of Chile in 1965 by using the geometric growth method and exponential method?
[Answer: 7.76 million and 7.59 million].

Assignment2 (Extrapolation): The annual growth rate for Chile between the period 1960 and 1970 was estimated at 2.4 percent per annum. What will Chile's population size be in 1980 on the assumption that the rate of 2.4 percent will continue into the 1980's?
[Answer: 10.80 million using exponential method].

Importance of Population Growth Rate:
(a) It is useful in estimating the rate of growth between censuses or in intercensal interval.
(b) It is useful in estimating size of population size of population in future at any time
(c) It is used in estimating size of population in a point of time between censuses.
(d) It is also useful in estimating time which it will take to reach a certain size in population

Note: Points connected to population growth rate are *interpolation* and *extrapolation*. *Interpolation* is a process of calculating size of population at a time between two dates at which their sizes are known i.e. *Pt* and *Po* are known or the average annual rate of increase 'r' between two dates is known.

Extrapolation is a process of estimating a value outside the range of values, which are given. In extrapolation, the two formulas, geometric growth or exponential growth method may be used to estimate the size of population at points of time in the future on the assumption that the growth rate 'r' is constant and will not change.

Doubling Time

Doubling time it consider about how long for the population to double itself. Growth expressed as a percentage is not very descriptive for many purposes. In calculating doubling time of the population it involves making the subject of the two formulas:

- Make n the subject of the formula

$$r = \frac{1}{n} ln \left(\frac{Pt}{Po} \right)$$

$$r \times n = \frac{1}{n} \times n \, ln \left(\frac{Pt}{Po} \right)$$

$$rn = ln \left(\frac{Pt}{Po} \right)$$

$$\frac{rn}{r} = \frac{ln \left(\frac{Pt}{Po} \right)}{r}$$

$$n = \frac{1}{r} ln \left(\frac{Pt}{Po} \right)$$

- For doubling time Pt = 2Po in the formula substituting Pt = 2Po.

$$n = \frac{1}{r} ln \left(\frac{2Pt}{Po} \right)$$

$$n = \frac{1}{r} ln2$$

$r = \sqrt[n]{\frac{Pt}{Po}} - 1$: Make **n** the subject of the formula for doubling time.

$$n = \frac{1}{r}$$

$$n = \frac{1}{r} \times \ln 2$$

$$\boldsymbol{n = \frac{\ln 2}{r}}$$

$$n = \frac{0.69314718}{0.029} = 23.90162692$$

$$= \boldsymbol{24\ years}$$

Note: ln2 =0.69314718; e = 2.72; r = 0.029; Pt = Po^{nxr}

Therefore: A quick way to obtain doubling time is to divide 70 by the growth rate (called law 70). Law 70: if a population is growing at a constant rate of 1% per year, it can be expected to double approximately every 70 years. If the rate of growth is 2% then the expected doubling time is $\frac{70}{2}$ or 35 year.

$$Doubling\ time = \frac{70}{Growth\ rate\ (\%)} = \frac{70}{2.9} = 24.1379$$

If its 2002 growth rate of 2.9 continued unchanged, Tanzania would double its population in about 24 years *(i.e. in the year 2002 + 24 = year 2026).*

OPTIMUM POPULATION

By definition, *optimum population* can be defined as an equal relationship between the available resources and the number of population in an area.

The size, distribution and structure of the population within a country must be viewed in relation to its natural resources and the techniques of production used by its people. The extent to which resources are used and the way in which they are used determine whether an area is under or over populated.

A country is said to have optimum population when the number of people in balance with the available resources. Optimum condition can only be maintained if the exploitation of new resources or the development of other forms of employment keeps pace with increases in population. If the population becomes too large, *the law of diminishing returns* begins to operate.

Once the optimum population has been reached, however, a further increase may increase production but at decreasing rate, so that output per capital declines. Under population and over population, therefore must be considered mainly in terms of the stage of development of the country concerned, and the standard by which this is measured.

OVER POPULATION

Overpopulation occurs when a population of a species exceeds the carrying capacity of its ecological niche. *Overpopulation* is a function of the number of individuals compared to the relevant resources, such as the water and essential nutrients they need to survive. It can result from an increase in births, a decline in mortality, an increase in immigration, or unsustainable biome and depletion of resources. The following are the *Indicators of over population:*

1. High population density.
2. High level of illiteracy.
3. Low science and technology.
4. Vulnerability of natural disaster.
5. Rapid increase of rural population.
6. Skewed distribution of agricultural land.
7. Lack of development of non-agricultural sector.
8. Lack of social development.

Causes of Overpopulation:

Decline in the Death Rate: At the root of overpopulation is the difference between the overall birth rate and death rate in populations. If the number of children born each year equals the number of adults that die, then the population will stabilize. Talking about overpopulation shows that while there are many factors that can increase the death rate for short periods of time, the ones that increase the birth rate do so over a long period of time. The discovery of agriculture by our ancestors was one factor that provided them with the ability to sustain their nutrition without hunting. This created the first imbalance between the two rates.

Better Medical Facilities: Technological advancement was perhaps the biggest reason why the balance has been permanently disturbed. Science was able to produce better means of producing food, which allowed families to feed more mouths. Medical science made many discoveries thanks to which they were able to defeat a whole range of diseases. Illnesses that had claimed thousands of lives till now were cured because of the invention of vaccines. Combining the increase in food supply with fewer means of mortality tipped the balance and became the starting point of overpopulation.

More Hands to Overcome Poverty: However, when talking about overpopulation we should understand that there is a psychological component as well. For thousands of years, a very small part of the population had enough money to live in comfort. The rest faced poverty and would give birth to large families to make up for the high infant mortality rate. Families that have been through poverty, natural disasters or are simply in need of more hands to work are major factor for overpopulation. As compared to earlier times, most of these extra children survive and consume resources that are not sufficient in nature.

Technological Advancement in Fertility Treatment: With latest technological advancement and more discoveries in medical science, it has become possible for couple who are unable to conceive to undergo fertility treatment methods and have their own babies. Today there are effective medicines which can increases the chance of conception and lead to rise in birth rate. Moreover, due to modern techniques pregnancies today are far safer.

Immigration: Many people prefer to move to developed countries like US, UK, Canada and Australia where best facilities are available in terms of medical, education, security and employment. The end result is that those people settle over there and those places become overcrowded. Difference between the number of people who are leaving the country and the number of people who are entering narrows down which leads to more demand of food, clothes, energy and homes. This gives rise to shortage of resources and accommodation. Though the overall population remains the same, it just affects the density of population making that place simply be overcrowded. Not only outside of the country or continent, also immigration might affect domestically internal the country itself.

Lack of Family Planning: Most developing nations have large number of people who are illiterate, live below the poverty line and have little or no knowledge about family planning. Getting their children married at an early age tends to increase the chances of producing more kids. Those people are unable to understand the harmful effects of overpopulation and lack of knowledge prompts them to avoid family planning measures.

Negative Effects of Overpopulation:
    (i)   Led to the lack of employment opportunities.
    (ii) High exploitation of the available resources, hence depletion of resources.
    (iii) Led to the shortage of food and water.
    (iv) Causes for the spread of diseases due to the high number of people in an area.
    (v) Poor standard of living and health to the people.
    (vi) High number of people influences environmental pollution and degradation.
    (vii) Occurrence of conflict over scarce resources.
    (viii) Increased in evils and crimes.

Positive Impacts of Overpopulation:
  (1) Availability of labor, both skilled and unskilled labor.
  (2) May lead to the advancement of science and technology.
  (3) Effective utilization of the available resources.
  (4) Presence of market to all products, due to the high population in relation to the demand.

UNDERPOPULATION

Under population refers to the low number of people in an area. Under population have the following indicators:
1. Low population growth rate.
2. The country experience high life expectancy.
3. High D.G.P.
4. Well developed technology and science.
5. There are rare natural disasters.
6. Small rural urban ratio.

Causes of Under Population:

1. Low birth rate and fertility rate.
2. Uses of birth control measures.
3. Increased death rate.
4. High emigration.
5. Poverty and economic hardship that lower life expectance of people.

Negative Effects of Under Population:
(1) Led to the underutilization of resources.
(2) Cause to the shortage of manpower.
(3) Inadequate of market due to low population.
(4) There is uneven distribution of population.

Positive Effects of Under Population:
1. No environmental pollution and degradation on under populated areas.
2. Abundance availability of employment opportunities.
3. Abundance availability of resources.
4. Low pressure on social amenities.
5. Low evils and crimes.
6. Adequate planning and implementation to the low population.

Why the Global Population Over Increasing?

The global population is increasing because of the following reasons:

(1) *Economic factor*: In Least Developing Countries most of the people recognize that children can be the source of labor in farms, small trade or sometime as the source of money when girl-children got married with high bride price.

(2) *Social factor:* Little use of birth control due to the low education, ignorance and negligence (especially in LDCs). Some tribes take as prestige in having many children, such that having six up to ten children in a family is normal. Early marriage; traditional beliefs and religion beliefs they condemns for the use of modern methods of birth control like condom among others.

(3) *Political factor*: Government failing to finance family planning programs due to the poor economic level of the nation.

Factors Influencing on Rapid Population Growth (Increase):

1. *Fertility rate*. Where there is high fertility there is high population growth like in Kenya. This is due to sex preferences, polygamist, and early marriage.

2. *Low mortality rate*. Where there is low mortality rate, there is high population growth and where there is high mortality, there is low population growth.

3. *Immigration.* Inflow of people from one place or country may lead to population growth.

4. *Cultural beliefs like.* Sex preferences, having many children as a sign of prestige, early marriage, polygamism, naming of relatives in all them they influence rapid population increase.

5. *Health services.* Improved health service has led to the decline in death rate. The life expectancy has been increasing and impact mortality rate has declined leading for the increase of fertility.

6. *Availability of food*. Presence of enough food, people increase reproductive capacity in the presence of food because people may not be worried to feed a high population hence increasing in reproduction.

7. *Modernization*. Early marriage and improved nutrition to the youth they became parents very early and hence they start getting children in teenage stage.

8. *Religion.* Some religions do not accept artificial method of birth control; saying that, they are quite abominable before God and hence they encourage or advocate natural methods like abstention from sex, which are less effective in the birth capacity.

9. *Economic factor*. Due to poverty people like to have many children so that, they can provide cheap labor. This by then was very common among the Nyamwezi and the Sukuma (not now days) in Tanzania.

10. *Political factor.* Poor policy in family planning that lack implementation strategies.

Qn: *(i) Assess for the advantages of population increase (rapid population growth).*

(ii) Discuss for the short coming of rapid population growth/population increase.

Impact of High Population Growth

A growing population can be an *asset* or a *liability* that is it can be positive or negative impacts as follows:

Positive Impacts:
 (1) Provide people for utilizing resources.
 (2) Encourage improvement of science and technology.
 (3) Population provides market for commodities.
 (4) Population enhances trading activities.

Negative Impacts:
 (i)   Population growth led to the intensive exploitative of natural resources.
 (ii) Lead to the soil erosion through farming activities and settlement establishment.
 (iii) Increase environmental pollution due to high pressure on the area.
 (iv) Increase of crimes and evils.
 (v)   Increase number of beggars especially in towns or cities.
 (vi) Lead to the inadequate of social services like education, water supply, medical services.
 (vii) May facilitate in spread of diseases both, STD's and communicable diseases.
 (viii) Cause for scarcity of land (shortage of land).
 (ix) May cause for shortage of food.

Qn. Rapid population growth in Tanzania it can therefore lead to the impact on Natural Resources? Discuss.

POPULATION PRESSURE

Population pressure is the same as population increase, high population growth, over population. The following are factors influencing population pressure (increase) in a place or an area:

a. Availability fertile soil.
b. Availability of minerals.
c. Availability of social services.
d. High fertility rate.
e. Scarcity of arable land.
f. Poor police of population control.

Impacts of population pressure *(refers to the effects of overpopulation):*

(a) Lead to inadequate in social services.
(b) Lead to unemployment.
(c) It can cause deforestation due to high demand of forest resource.
(d) Can cause to the outbreak of disease.
(e) Lead to the shortage of resources.
(f) Cause for environmental pollution and destruction.

CHAPTER 13:

POPULATION MIGRATION

Sometime population migration termed as *population movement. Population migration* refers to population movement from one place to another for permanent or temporary change of residence. Population migration can be in term of the followings:

(a) Voluntary and involuntary migration (push and pull factors for migration)
(b) Short term and long term migration.
(c) Internal and external/international (inter-region migration)
(d) Temporally and permanently migration.
(e) Large and small scale migration.

Population migration also can be categorized into two:
1. According to time;
(i) Permanent migration
(ii) Temporary migration

2. According to locality;
(i) Rural-rural migration
(ii) Urban-urban migration
(iii) Rural-urban migration
(iv) Urban-rural migration

Therefore, population movement involved by or influenced by pull factors and push factors. Pull factors and push factors can be physical, economic, social, political and Biological factors. Push factors influence for emigration while pull factors influence for immigration.

Push and Pull Factors of Population migration:
(1) Physical factor or natural factors:
a. *Climate:* Moderate temperature with enough rainfall do attract or pull people to immigrate in an area, while harsh temperature with poor rainfall (drought) tend to push or force people to emigrate from an area.

b. *Edaphic (soil) factor:* Area with fertile or good soil tends to pull or attract people to immigrate, while poor and unfertile soil tends to push or force people to emigrate.

c. *Availability precious metal:* The area with minerals acts as a pull factor to immigrate, like in Geita, Kahama, Mwadui and Merelani in Tanzania.

d. *Presence of Natural Hazards*: Like earth quakes, flood, drought, volcanic eruption and other storms. Here people are forced or pushed away, but in the area or place with absence of natural hazard act as a pull or attraction to the people to immigrate in such area this area.

(2) Biological factors.
o The area which is free of diseases and pests attract people to immigrate, while the area or place with presence disease and pests, people tends to emigrate in an area.

(3) Economic factors (hope of wealth And work for income and living).
Lack of income opportunities and employment opportunities in the area, people are pushed to move to the place where there are these opportunities for human and economic development. This situation tends to cause rural-urban migration in the country.

(4) Social factors.
Presence of relatives, social services on the area attracts people, while in absence of relatives and social services; people may not attend or live in such area.

(5) Political factors.
Peace political system, (political freedom), political stability, Good government policy for settlement schemes, attract people to live in a such place, while in the place with political instability with presence of civil wars, tribe wars, religious wars and harsh political system and policy that discourage people to establish settlement in the area.

People are seemed to be pushed away to establish their residence and settlement in such places. Sometimes there is a forced migration under the influence of the government itself for different purposes as villagization, national parks and investment establishment.

Characteristics of Migration:

(a) Migration is selective:
- ✓ In terms of age – young people aged from 20 up to 34 years old are more mobile due to economic reasons.
- ✓ In terms of sex or gender – male are more mobile in a larger distance while female move short distance in rural–urban migration.

(b) Most of migrants are poor since they move to search for economic opportunities.

(c) Most migrants travel in a specific distance to reach the aimed area.

(d) The number of migrants decreases while the distance is increasing in along.

(e) Migration is two way process due to the movement of opposite direction of migrants.

(f) Migration occurs in stages – short movement from one place leaves a chance to be filled by other population from beyond.

Eight Laws of Revenstein in Migration (1885)

1. There is a process of absorption whereby people immediately surround a rapidly growing town move into it and gapes they have are filled by migrants more distant areas and so on until the attractive force (pull factor) is spent.

2. There is a process of dispersion which is the inverse of absorption

3. Most of migrants move only a short distance.

4. Each migration flow produces a compensatory counter flow.

5. Long distance migrants go to one of the great centres of commerce and industries.

6. Natives of the town are less migratory than those from rural areas.

7. Economic factors are the main causes of migration.

8. Females are more migratory than males within the kingdom of their birth, but males are frequently venture beyond

Types of Migration

There are two main types of migration; internal and external migration:

(1) International (external) migration.

International migration is the movement of people from one country or continent to another. It can be permanent (long term) or temporary (short term). All external migration, however, are not voluntary likes slaves, refugees etc. External migration has the following causes:

(a) Chain migration (this is through sequence of events like wars).
(b) Short term contract (contract from one country or continent to another).
(c) Brain drain (is the movement of highly-qualified or skilled people to another country searching for employment).
(d) Tourism (movement of tourists to another country for different purposes).

(2) Internal migration.

Internal migration refers to the movement of people from one place to another within a country. This can be urban to rural migration or rural to urban migration. This also can be involuntary or voluntary in-migration and out-migration. Internal migration is caused by:

(a) Long term due to moving of government office.
(b) Family matters (moving to see the family like who are working away with their family member).
(c) Permanent shift from the old place to the new place of residence
(d) Short term migration that caused for trade, holiday etc.

Four (4) patterns of internal migration commonly in Africa:

(i)   Rural to urban migration.
(ii)   Urban to rural migration.
(iii) Urban to urban migration.
(iv)   Rural to rural migration.

1: Rural to Urban Migration

This is the migration of people from rural to urban areas. Most of migrants in these are youths and energetic people and especially are males. There are reasons that lead rural-urban migration:

- People do move from urban areas in the expectation of getting job opportunities.
- For the matter of getting better social services.
- Getting entertainment.
- Getting tertiary education and schooling.
- For business activities.
- Getting access with Medias and press.

Impacts of Rural – Urban Migration

(a) In the source (in rural area) or departure:

    (i)   Lead to rural depopulation.

    (ii)   Lead to economic decline.

    (iii)   Shortage of food (food crisis) due to poor agriculture performance.

    (iv)   Breakage of family.

    (v)   Room for environmental conservation (positive impacts).

(a) In the destination (in urban Areas):

    (i)   Tends to cause over population in an area.

    (ii)   Inadequate of social service e.g. supply of pure and safe water.

    (iii)   Leads to cultural deterioration due to high interaction of people.

    (iv)   Lead to environmental pollution and degradation.

    (v)   May facilitate for increase of crimes.

    (vi)   Decline of industries due to low supply of raw materials from rural areas (especially agricultural raw materials).

    (vii)   Emergence of street children and beggars.

    (viii) Led to the supply of labor in rural areas (positive impact).

Ways of Addressing or Solving the Problems of Rural-Urban Migration:

- Reduction and elimination of income differentials between rural and urban areas.
- Enacting strictly policy that restricts unnecessary movement of people from rural to urban.
- Creation of many small centers in rural areas as that found in urban areas.

- Improvement of transport and communication system in rural area.
- Provision of good social services in rural areas as those found in urban centers.

2: Urban to Rural Migration

This is the migration of people from urban to rural areas. Reasons for rural-urban migration are:

- People escaping and avoid noises and air pollutions in urban area.
- People tend to go back in rural areas after retirement.
- For unskilled labor that faced with difficulties in urban areas tends to go in rural areas.
- Outbreak of terrible diseases in urban area.
- Lack of space to allocate large scale of economic activities like large plantations, ranches among others.

Problems that Caused By Urban-Rural Migration:

(1) Outbreak of conflict with old residents due to land deprivation.
(2) Problems of house e.g. high price increase in house in rural areas.
(3) Lead to land degradation due to deforestation and soil erosion.
(4) Cultural interference in the urban areas hence outbreak of conflict.
(5) Increase in pollution due to the increase of number of people
(6) Increase in crime, which are common in urban areas.

Advantage of Urban-Rural Migration:

a. It can stimulate exploitation of resource.
b. Reduce burden to the government in provision of social services in urban areas.
c. Reduce population pressure in towns.
d. Facilitate the general development in rural areas, hence reduction in economic gap between rural and urban areas.
e. It reduces of environmental degradation and pollution.

<u>*On:*</u> *By giving definition, impacts on origin or departure and impacts 0n the destination; discuss for the following questions*:

        a. Rural – Rural Migration
        b. Urban – Urban Migration

General Effects of Population Migration:

Negative effects: Depopulation spread of diseases, draining of skills and technology, retard of production, decline of manpower and culture destruction.

Positive effects: Technological diffusion due to interaction of people, economic development. People remit money to their areas of origin, facilitate population distribution and finally facilitate special interaction and socialization.

CHAPTER 14:

POPULATION DATA

Population data is the information pertaining to population in terms of economy, social and demographic matters. Population data are obtained from government institutions, international institutions, UN statistical demographic year book, World Bank demographic reports, and population reference bureau data sheets among others. Population Data have the following two sources:
  (i)   Secondary source of data.
  (ii) Primary source of data.

Primary Source of Data

Primary source of data are data that obtained from first hand data. Primary source of data alternatively it is known as traditional source of data. Example of primary source of data area:
  (a) Population census.
  (b) Demographic sample survey.
  (c) Vital registration.

Secondary Source of Data

Secondary source of data are data that obtained from other findings (second hand data). Secondary source of data it is known as non-traditional source of data. Examples of secondary source of data are:
  (a) School register.
  (b) Labor register.
  (c) Medical records.
  (d) Baptismal records.
  (e) Religion or parish records.
  (f) Maternal clinic and child welfare.
  (g) Published reports and unpublished reports as well as statistical abstract.

Note: In developing countries, demographic data comes mainly from census, sample survey and vital registration.

Characteristics of Population (Demographic) Data:

a) Obtained through observation and recording events which found on external world.

b) The primary statistical units of the observation on demographic data are individual and the secondary is the family or household.

c) Politically, the populations of an area determine the level of electoral representation in the parliament through demographic data.

d) Helps to establish project under the obtained demographic data.

e) Population data should be systematically collected, sufficient reliable to reflect the real event on a specific area.

I. SAMPLE SURVEY.

Sample survey is the system of collecting statistical information about population which involves a selection of a suitable represented size in the community to form population that provides information on death, birth and migration.

Its purpose is to represent information of the area concerned such as ward, district, and region within a particular territory. A sample survey can be into:

1. *Single round sample survey*: involve only one interview with respondent
2. *Multi round sample survey*: involves interviewing the same respondent several times.

Advantages of sample survey:
1. It is simple to conduct and administer.
2. It is more flexible than census as it allows a wide range of questions.
3. It is less expensive compound to census as it involves only a sample
4. Allow more detailed information to be collected

Disadvantages of sample survey:
1. Suffer from sampling error due to selection of sample to represent the majority.
2. Not easier to compare the data obtained from sample survey from other countries
3. It is poor in coverage, due to small population and areas considered

4. Not accurate due to generalization of data from the population

II. VITAL REGISTRATION

Vital registration is the way of collecting population data through death registration, birth registration and marriage registration. In addition, this is the basic source of data of a population. Now day in Tanzania vital registration is done by RITA (Registration and
Insolvent Trusteeship Agency).

In the other way vital or civil registration is the system by which a government records the vital events of its citizens and residents. Vital registration creates legal documents which may be used to establish and protect the civil rights of individuals, as well as providing a source of data which may be compiled to give vital statistics.

In contrast to censuses, which collect information on every member of a population at a single point in time, vital registration systems collect information on individuals as demographic events occur. You may also see 'vital registration' called 'civil registration', which is the preferred term of the UN Many vital registration systems record births, deaths, foetal deaths, marriages, divorces and adoptions, as well as recording information on the individual who experiences the event, such as age, religion, occupation etc. These data are then compiled into vital statistics bulletins

Reasons to why most of events are not recorded in Vital Registration (in African countries):
   (i) Passive in nature of registration system.
   (ii) Costs involved in records.
   (iii) Birth and death occurring at home cannot be easily registered or recorded.
   (iv) High illiteracy rate.
   (v) Lack of skilled labour to registration staff.
   (vi) Most of people are not seeing the advantage of these records.
   (vii) Most of people are located in urban areas (district, region and cities) and not in villages.

Usefulness and advantage of Vital Registration:
   a. To check correct age of children for starting school.
   b. To know causes of accident and death of a person.

c. To provide health service needed to the population.

d. People to have legal rights to their nation.

Disadvantage of Vital Registration:

(1) It is very expensive since it needs permanent infrastructure and personnel.

(2) It is the second hand information given by people that might be seemed to be not concerned with events (of death, birth and marriage).

(3) Poor coverage due to the lack of registration centers and registration officer.

(4) No legal follow-up (no information of laws).

(5) Registration sometimes are done by other officers who do it as an extra duty, like Nurses, hence information can be incomplete.

The advantages of vital registration can be divided into two categories:

- Legal
- Statistical

Legal advantages to vital registration

When a demographic event is registered, legal documents are issued as proof of this event. This confers a range of legal benefits upon the holder.

- Registration of a birth establishes and protects the identity of an individual, and confers citizenship upon them. This legal recognition entitles the individual to state services and protection from exploitation.

- The establishment of a legal identity (and the corresponding legal documents) allows individuals to vote, to be registered for education, and to move between countries (through the ability to apply for a passport).

- In many countries valid death certificates are required before a burial permit can be obtained.

- Valid death certificates are required before life assurance payments will be made.

- In the event of a death, marriage certificates and birth certificates showing parentage are important in securing inheritance and land rights.

Statistical advantages to vital registration

In addition to legal benefits for individuals, there are benefits for society which result from the availability of high quality, up to date information on births, deaths and causes of deaths.

- Continuous registration of births and deaths allows for future population estimates.

- Death registration and detailed cause of death classification are important for understanding the health of a population. This can then be used to formulate and prioritize effective public health policies and interventions.

- The same information allows for monitoring of the effectiveness of public health interventions. This allows governments to ensure that tax money is spent in effective ways, and gives accountability to aid donors that donated money is improving the health of a population in the way that it was intended.

- Vital registration also allows for monitoring progress towards targets, such as the Millennium Development Goals (MDGs). Without continuous registration of vital events, it is difficult to know whether progress is being made and whether the target is likely to be reached by 2015.

Quality of Vital Registration Systems

The table below shows the qualities of vital registration system:

	Measure
Accurate	In order for a vital registration system to be accurate, it should have: - High coverage (% of population covered) - High completeness (% of events included) - Low levels of missing data - Low usage of ill-defined categories used as cause of death - Low numbers of improbable classifications - Consistency between cause of death and general mortality
Relevant	In order for a vital registration system to be relevant, it should give: - Routine tabulations - Small area statistics
Comparable	Vital registration systems should be: - Comparable over time - Comparable across space

Timely	For vital statistics to be useful in informing health policy, they must be: • Produced regularly • Have little time between collection, compilation and publication
Accessible	For vital statistics to be accessible, they should be: • Produced in a number of different media formats • Provide information about the data (i.e. collection method, definitions, manner of presentation, potential for error etc.) • Provide a responsive user service to distribute data, clarify queries and engage with data providers

Adapted from Mahapatra et al. (2007)

On some levels, as suggested earlier, it makes sense to expand the number of questions asked of individuals and households – the marginal cost of adding an additional question is relatively small compared with the overall scale of the census project. However, it is not uncommon for a form of political horse-trading to occur whereby if one ministry or agency secures the right to field a question or questions in the census (e.g. on access to piped water), another ministry may argue that it should also be entitled to field questions (e.g. on access to mobile telephone).

The result of such a process can result in long, cumbersome and unwieldy census instruments. In turn, this may compromise the overall quality of the data collected as respondents and enumerators may become disaffected with the length of the questionnaire. In addition, the extra questions will add to the complexity of the data set and any editing performed on the data, on the size of the data files that result, as well as increasing the time taken to process and collate the information.

In general, it is preferable to keep the number of questions asked in a census down to a minimum, focusing on those data required to enumerate the population and on variables that require large sample sizes to measure accurately. The results from the enumeration can be used as the sampling frame for specific and much more detailed enquiries that can be conducted on a sample basis on a much smaller portion of the population. Examples of such enquiries would be Demographic and Health Surveys;

What Information Should be Collected in Vital Registration?

The United Nations (UN Department of Economic and Social Affairs, Statistics Division 2001) lists information which should be considered high priority when registering vital events. These are presented in the table below. The full UN report lists further characteristics of interest which are not considered high priority, as well as further information on the definition of each of the topics.

	Recommended High Priority Topics
Births	• Date of occurrence of birth
	• Date of registration
	• Place of occurrence of birth
	• Place of registration
	• Type of birth (i.e. single, twin, multiple etc.)
	• Attendant at birth
	• Characteristics of the child
	• Sex
	• Birth weight
	• Characteristics of the mother
	• Age (or date of birth)
	• Marital status
	• Educational attainment
	• Place of usual residence
	• Children born alive to the mother during her entire lifetime
	• Children born alive to the mother and still living
	• Foetal deaths to the mother during her entire lifetime
	• Date of previous live birth
	• Date of marriage
	• Characteristics of the father

	• Age (or date of birth)
	• Marital status
	• Educational attainment
	• Place of usual residence
Deaths	• Date of occurrence
	• Date of registration
	• Place of occurrence
	• Place of registration
	• Cause of death
	• Certifier
	• Age (or date of birth)
	• Sex
	• Marital status
	• Place of usual residence
	• Place of usual residence of the mother (for deaths under one year of age)

A note on registering cause of death

Some other terms associated with vital events registration are live birth, sexual union, parturition, foetal death, still birth, divorce and abortion (spontaneous and induce) Registration of cause of death, as certified by a medical practitioner, has the clear benefit of providing a health profile of a population. This allows priorities to be set in public health, and for policies to be formulated. If accompanied by information on characteristics of the decedent, such as age, sex, occupation, ethnicity etc., it is possible to identify mortality differentials between groups.

The cause of death which is used for statistical purposes should be the underlying cause of death, i.e. the disease or incident which initiated the chain of events leading to the death. This should be coded according to the rules and guidelines outlined in the latest revision of the *International Statistical Classification of Diseases and Health Related Problems* (ICD). Coding according to these rules allows for valid international comparisons.

One of the criteria for a vital registration system to be considered high quality is that the data it produces must be "timely". This usually refers to the efficiency of the departments in charge of collecting, collating and publishing the statistics and their ability to produce reports regularly and within a useful timeframe.

However it is worth noting that the timeliness of the data produced is also reliant on individuals reporting events soon after they have occurred. In many countries it is a legal requirement for the event to be reported within a set timeframe. For example, in the UK all births must be reported within 42 day. However, in many developing countries vital events might be notified to authorities many years after the event has occurred. Of the births occurring in South Africa in 1998, only 58% of the births registered within five years were registered during the year of birth or the following year.

III. POPULATION CENSUS

Census is the official counting of a country's population. Census is also defined as the process of counting, collecting, compiling demographic, economic and social data to the specific time to all people in the country.

United Nation's definition of a census:

"The total process of collecting, compiling, analyzing, and publishing or otherwise disseminating demographic, economic and social data pertaining to all persons in a country or in a well-delineated part of a country at a specified time." There are several aspects of this definition that are worth emphasizing.

1. This definition refers to the "**total process**". It not sufficient to simply collect and collate information in a census. The data collected must also be analyzed, published and disseminated.

2. The scope of a census encompasses **demographic, economic and social data**. Thus a census will often seek to collect more than just a simple headcount of the population. The reasons for this relates to the logistics of the exercise: if one is going to try to individually enumerate each person in a population, the marginal cost of collecting additional information (on income, education, housing etc.) is low, although will lead to an increase in the length of (and hence time taken to complete) the census instrument. The implications of this are discussed in a later section. Often the census is referred to as a Population and Housing Census to emphasise the broader ambitions of the census.

3. The census aims for **universality**, that is, to enumerate all people in a population. This is less simple than it may seem. The problems associated with attempting to define and count "all the people within a population" will be discussed in the following pages.

4. The census aims for **simultaneity** - it seeks to produce a snapshot of the population at a point in time. With the exception of very small and compact populations, it is usually impossible to actually enumerate a population on a single date. In many countries, census enumeration takes place over a number of weeks. To this end, censuses usually have a defined 'census date' for which responses are elicited, regardless of when the questions are actually put to the respondent. Households are asked to recall the people who slept in the house or who were usual members of the household on the census date. Births and deaths that occurred between the census date and the date of enumeration (when the household was actually counted) should be omitted.

Back Ground of Census

Censuses have been used for thousands of years. Initially, their prime purpose was for levying taxes or raising armies. Egypt, 5000 years ago, sought to produce a list of households and household members every second year.

Imperial Rome, around the beginning of the Christian era, sought to count the population every five years, largely for taxation. The modern census, however, evolved in Europe in the 1600s as an aspect of 'political arithmetic' whereby countries sought to quantify the military and fiscal power of the state.

Sweden's first complete census occurred in 1749, with other European countries following soon in the next hundred years. The first census in the United States occurred in 1790, and the constitution mandates a census to be held every ten years; the results are fundamental to the allocation of seats in the (lower) House of Representatives.

Characteristics or Features of Census:

(1) Universality: census is universality because it involves all people in the nation of a specific territory (coverage).

(2) Simultaneity: census is defined for a different time that takes place in a specific time interval of period.

(3) Confidentiality: Secret data for each individual should be kept during a censuring time.

(4) Sponsored by government: census is mostly sponsored by government so as to be conducted.

(5) Costly in time and money: all stages and processes of census involve time and money.

(6) Individuality: Individual is primary enumerated and recorded his or her data in censuring time. There should be physical counting of people rather than by proxy.

(7) Defined periodicity: Involves specific time interval especially 5 or 10 years of time interval.

(8) Regularity: Censuses consider a regular definite interval.

Methods of Enumeration of Census:

(i) Canvasser or enumerator method: refers to the official and enumeration of each house and collecting data for each individual.

(ii) House hold method: Here questionnaires are sent in the house hold in advance of the house to find out the data.

Method of Census Taking:

(1) *De facto*: A person is counted where he or she found in the night.

(2) *De jure:* Person is counted based on the permanent residence.

Types of Censuses

Types of census can be categorized according to approach of taking censuses or according to the time interval.

1. According To the Approach, Census can be:

(i) De jure census: Is the one which people are counted according to their usual place of residence. Only permanent members of household are counted. This method is disadvantaged by regarding people as they are static while they are dynamic.

(ii) De facto: Is the one in which people are counted wherever they are found on the day of enumeration. All people who stayed in the household for the night are counted.

2. According To the Time Interval, census can be:

(i) <u>Quiquenial census</u>: Refers to the census that carried out after every five years.

(ii) <u>Decennial census</u>: It is the type of census carried after every ten years.

Advantages of de facto:
1. It is clear and simple because it involves only those physically present in the census's night are to be counted.
2. Avoid the distinction between temporary and permanent residence.
3. It is suitable for developing countries where majority are illiterate because can be interviewed by census enumerators.
4. It is time saving since the time used to enumerate is short in obtaining the information.
5. Not easier for manipulation, as everyone is counted according to where he or she is found.

Disadvantages of de facto:
1. People like pilots, sailors and in transits may miss enumeration when they will be on work during night before census.
2. It is very costly in term of financial and human resources.
3. It may give wrong impression of population size for areas with high migration and seasonal mobility.
4. Enumeration is fast hence may occur unnoticed mistakes.

Advantages of de jure:
1. It is technically free from the time limit or seasonal mobility or migration.
2. May be suitable for people flying, floating or in transits because can easily enumerated based on usual and legal residence.
3. Due to abundance time, lot of question can be asked so as to get accurate information.

Disadvantages of de jure:
1. It requires real definition of permanent residence.
2. People with temporary residence cannot be counted.
3. May not reflect the size of the population in the country.
4. Difficult to count people with permanent address.
5. There is always some uncertainty about what should be considered to people's usual residence.

Contrast Between De Facto and De Jure Enumerations

An important distinction is often drawn between populations that are enumerated on a defacto (Latin, for 'in actual fact') and a de jure (Latin for 'in law') basis.

- ***De facto*** – The population is enumerated where it is found, regardless of the respondent's usual place of residence.

- ***De jure*** – The respondent is enumerated at their usual place of residence, regardless of where they stayed on the census date.

Objectives or Purposes of Census:

(a) To provide complete account of all members of the country by age and sex.

(b) To obtained the detailed statistics on the size, nature and distribution of labor force.

(c) To determine the literacy and illiteracy rate of the population in the relevant age group.

(d) To provide and get social and economic information on the household and the county in general.

(e) To provide the general picture of the all places of the villages in the country and persons.

(f) To determine the total number of the population in the country hence to plan for the social service provision.

Advantages of census

- The coverage aims to be universal

- The census provides an important sampling frame for subsequent surveys and studies

- The census can serve as a useful tool for 'nation-building', by involving the entire population

- Census data avoids the sampling errors that can occur with sample data

- Censuses provide data for small areas, such as districts and counties, which is vital for the planning of services

Disadvantages of census

- The size and complexity of the exercise means that the content and quality control efforts may be limited
- The cost of carrying out a census means that most countries can pursue an enumeration only every ten years
- There is usually a significant delay between when the data are collected and the results released. Typically this delay is between 18 months to two years, and means that the census only offers a snapshot of the population at some point in the past
- Censuses are easily politicized – either by groups who feel that they might be systematically undercounted by the exercise, or by parties with a vested interest in seeking to ensure that their group's population is found to be larger than that of other groups

Importance of Population Census

The fundamental purpose of the census at a glance:

1. Provide the facts essential to government for policy-making, planning and administration.
2. Decision-making that facilitates the development of socio-economic policies -enhance the welfare of the population.
3. Provides important data for the analysis and appraisal of the changing patterns of rural or urban movement and concentration, the development of urbanized areas, geographical distribution of the population according to such variables as occupation and education, as well as the socio-economic characteristics of the population and the labor force.
4. Aids in the decision-making processes of the private sector. Population size and characteristics influence the location of businesses and services that satisfy the needs of the target population.

How do we Use the Census Data?

Data of population census are used for:

1. Development planning purposes

2. Estimation of levels and variations in population and housing characteristics

3. Estimating sources of labor force

4. Identifying the role of women and their economic and social standing

5. Learning about special population groups

6. Use for research purposes

7. Use for economic purposes. National development requires a well-organized statistical system allowing planners to work on the broad set of statistical indicators that are indispensable for the development and improvement of planning. In order to involve the statistical system in the planning and delivery of the designed and desired statistical data

Who Can Make Use of the Census Information?

Everyone inside the country or outside it can use the census data; accordingly, they serve for a great   variety of uses. A great deal of information is available on the CBS website and on the sites of international organizations. Additional information can be acquired by a direct application to the CBS.

The following are examples of possible users and uses:

A.   *Government ministries* - the census data are available to decision-makers as a basis for setting policies in various fields: education, health, and welfare, dealing with various levels in the population, housing and development, transportation and other services.

Examples:

▪ Planning and provision of services in the educational system according to the needs of the   population and the age of the children.
▪ Planning of public transportation and transportation infrastructure, according to the projected   amount of traffic in the area.
▪ Planning a system of assistance to the needy.
▪ Development of infrastructure according to the needs of the population.
▪ Channeling of budgets to local authorities.

B.   *Local authorities* - the census data are available to decision-makers in local authorities as a basis for setting local policies in each locality, according to the needs of its population. The data assist in learning about the characteristics of neighborhoods and populations in the localities.

Examples:

▪ Examining the need for establishing early childhood services and public gardens in areas   where there is a high percentage of children of this age.
▪ Using the data in determining municipal tax areas adapted to the characteristics of the   population.

C.   ***Bodies of research*** - conducting research based on census data. Population censuses are an important resource for research on trends in the composition of a population and its distribution, as well as a source of analysis and assessment of the changes occurring in the population, and construction of a forecast regarding the directions of its development.

Examples of research:

▪ Means of transportation to work and socio-economic status in Israel.
▪ Migration from development towns (from the periphery to the center or from one locality in the   periphery to another).
▪ Changes in education and fertility patterns of Moslem women in Israel.

D.   ***Private and public companies*** - conducting research for purposes of acquiring commercial information to serve as a basis for market research, assessment of the demand for products and services, and assessment of the supply of personnel.

Examples:

▪ Identifying concentrations of old structures, by companies dealing in structure restoration.
▪ Allocation of the maximum support by the State Lottery to various localities; which is   determined, among other things, based on indices developed from census data.

E.   ***Journalists*** - acquisition of information from the census data, on subjects which serve for conducting research and as backgrounds for articles.

Examples:

. Acquisition of information on socio-economic characteristics of localities, for an article on the   state of education in them.

. Acquisition of information on the average wage in various localities and comparing it with the level   of development in them.

F.   <u>**Students and pupils**</u> - writing seminar papers and research projects for graduate degrees, based on data from the population and housing census; writing papers for school.

Examples:

. Use of data on areas in which there is a high concentration of families blessed with many   children, for research projects in sociology.

G.   <u>*The general public*</u> - use of data in a wide variety of many fields, relevant to each individual

Examples:

. Use of information on a residential area, in order to decide on a change of residence.

. Acquiring information on the subject of employment and wages by occupation, which may   direct youngsters in their decision to choose a field of study.

. Identification of locations suitable for opening a business, by the self-employed.

Population censuses also constitute the principal source of records for use as a sampling frame for the household surveys during the years between censuses.

Limitation of Census:

a) Low literacy level among the people, limit the process of under taking census

b) Poor coordination in the process of under taking census between the people and enumerators.

c) Poor coordination in the process of under taking census between the enumerators and the respondents (poor communication).

d) Poor framing of questions creates fear among the individuals.

e) Political instability of a place/country.

f) Transport problem to the remoteness area also limit the process of under taking census.

g) Problem of misreporting the information e.g. Age and population characteristics
h) Shortage of useful material and facilities.
i) Poor payment to the enumerators
j) Omissions of some members especially for those found absent hence poor coverage.
k) The expenses in conducting census through training manpower, wages, and buying facilities/materials.

Summary

Population data can be gathered from a number of sources. This session has outlined the primary sources, their advantages and disadvantages, and outlined some options for when data from these sources are not available.

Censuses are the main source of data on population stock. Ideally held every ten years, they involve an enumeration of the entire population of a nation and often include the collection of additional information on social and economic characteristics.

However, censuses can only provide a "snapshot" of a moment in time, and by the time all the data has been collated, analyzed and disseminated, it will often be a number of years out of data. Furthermore, censuses are expensive, time-consuming and require large amounts of man-power.

Because of these disadvantages, a number of countries have moved towards population registers. These collate and link information from vital registration and administrative registers, and provide an up-to-date and near instantaneous profile of the population.

Vital registration – the registering of vital events, such as births, deaths and marriages – remains the ideal source of information on demographic events. However, many countries in the world do not have a high quality system for vital registration, if they have a system at all.

In these situations it may be possible to use alternative methods to estimate the number of demographic events, such as sample registration, demographic surveillance sites and verbal autopsy. Nevertheless, these should be seen as interim measures, with a comprehensive system of vital registration still seen as the ultimate goal

Errors in Population Data

Types of errors in population data are into two: coverage error and content error. *Error of coverage* occurs when events go without registration e.g. birth, death, marriage. *Errors of content occur*s when information is incorrect, incomplete recorded due to second hand information and misrecording or misreporting.

Therefore, there five principles in source of errors: *responds source of error, editing process source of error, data entry source of error, coding process source of errors* and *recorders source of error* (when recorders are not well trained). In orders to detect errors in population data, there are two ways: *comparison of tabulated* and *comparison of individual data.*

CHAPTER 15:

POPULATION POLICY

Policy refers to the action of plan to guide decision and action, while population policy is the statement, law, regulation enacted so as to attain some demographic goals. Population policy considers the relationship between population and development. Population policy is categorized into two major groups:

(i) Explicit population policy
(ii) Implicit population policy

1. Explicit Population Policy: *r*efers to the policy statement issued by government to control population growth and raise the living standard of the people. Explicit population policy is well stipulated and strictly followed or reinforced. Under explicit population policy there are some penalties given to those who do not follow the policy.

2. Implicit Population Policy: refers to the policy, law, regulation or statement which may have direct or indirect effect on population growth. Implicit population policy is not elaborated, as explicit population policy, since it is unclear and cannot be easily understood leading to the failure in terms of implementation.

The differences between implicitly and explicitly policy are as follows:

S/N	*Explicity Policy*	*Implicity Policy*
01	The documents or statements are clear	The document or statements are not clear
02	Adherence to the statements or Regulation is always strict.	Adherences to the statements or regulation are sometime not strict.
03	The origin may be the pre-existing laws and dedication by parties or other laws.	They may not be a result of pre-existing laws or part of declaration.
04	The stipulation of the statement is always precise	The stipulation of statement is sometime not precise and exact to the point in

and exact to the point in question	questions.

Other Categories of Population Policy:

1. Expansive population policy: is the population policy that encourages the expansion of population by ordering families to raise the rate of population. Also the policy is called *Nationalism population policy*. An example of such policy is, *"Mother Heroine"* in the former Soviet Union.

2. Restrictive population policy. It is the population policy that restricts growth and increase of population. Also this population policy is known as *Anti-Nationalism population policy.* An example this policy is *"One-child population policy"* in China.

Characteristics of Population Policy:

(i) Selective: Population policies are selective; cover only small or specific demographic factors where the regulation is intended.

(ii) Explicit: The policies of population are explicitly because the policy becomes the document or clear statement issued by the government department
.

(iii) Implicit: Also population policies are characterized by being implicitly because; such policies have direct or indirect impact on the population grown. Due to being not understood or well elaborated, hence implicit population policies may lead to their own failures in implementation.

Qn: Highlight the differences between Explicit and implicit population policies.

Criteria for a Good Population Policy:

1. It should be based on the philosophy of respect to human life.

2. It should embody the concept of family planning which is concerned not only with the growth of population but also with the quality of life.

3. It should be an integral part of the countries development plan.

4. It should solicit the use and expertise of practitioners in the field of education, social welfare, demography, mass communication, and other related ideas.

5. It should involve the support of both the government and voluntary agencies.

CASE STUDY: POPULATION POLICY OF CHINA

In 1950's China had a philosophy of a large population gives a strong nation. This philosophy led to high birth rate. In 1960's every three years, China's population increased by 55 million. The country then introduced family planning programmes. In the 1970's the average family members were too many. It then started a new family planning programme of two children per family.

1. The 1979 China Population Policy

1979, China introduced one child per family policy. This policy enabled citizens to be given free education, priority housing, pension and family benefit. The family which had a second child could not have these benefits; they also faced fines of up to 15% of the family's income.

The marriage ages for men were 22 years and for women were 20. When the couples were intending for marriage, they were required to apply for permission from the state as well as when they intended to have a child.

Women who had second pregnancies were forced to have abortion. Family planning officers started visiting work place and homes to ensure that families fallowed the rules.

2. The Stipulation in Explicit Population Policies.

These policies are clear and easy to be fallowed enforced. For example China assured a policy of this kind where the limit to the number of children per marriage couple was set and both incentives and penalties to the complaints and clearly stipulated.

One Child Policy in China

The one child policy, a part of the family planning policy was a population control policy of China which was introduced between 1978 and 1980 and began to be formally phased out in 2015. The policy allowed many exceptions and ethnic minorities were exempt. In 2007, 36% of China's population was subject to a strict one-child restriction. An additional 53% were allowed to have a second child if the first child was a girl.

The policy was enforced at the provincial level through fines that were imposed based on the income of the family and other factors. "Population and Family Planning Commissions" exist at every level of government to raise awareness and carry out registration and inspection work.

The policy was introduced in 1978 and enacted/implemented as a temporary measure on September 18, 1980 to curb a then-surging population and limit the demands for water and other resources as well as to alleviate social, economic and environmental problems in China. Demographers are not clear how much reduction happened solely because of the policy.

Administration of the policy

The one-child policy was managed by the National Population and Family Planning Commission under the central government since 1981. The Ministry of Health of the People's Republic of China and the National Health and Family Planning Commission were made defunct and a new single agency National Health and Family Planning Commission took over national health and family planning policies in 2013. The agency reports to the State Council

Relaxation

The one-child policy was originally designed to be a one-generation policy. It was enforced at the provincial level and enforcement varied; some provinces had relaxed the restrictions. After Henan loosened the requirement, the majority of provinces and cities permitted two parents who were 'only children' themselves to have two children.

In November 2013, following the Third Plenum of the 18th Central Committee of the Chinese Communist Party, China announced the decision to relax the one-child policy. Under the new policy, families could have two children if one parent is an only child. This mainly applied to urban couples, since there were very few rural only children due to long-standing exceptions to the policy for rural couples. In rural areas, families are allowed two children without incurring penalties. The one-child limit has mostly been enforced in densely populated urban areas, and implementation varies from location to location.

Beginning in 1987, official policy granted local officials the flexibility to make exceptions and allow second children in the case of "practical difficulties" (such as cases in which the father is a disabled serviceman) or when both parents are single children, and some provinces had other exemptions worked into their policies as well. In most areas, families are allowed to apply to have a second child if their first-born is a daughter. Furthermore, families with children with disabilities have different policies and families whose first child suffers from physical disability, mental illness, or intellectual disability are allowed to have more children.

Children born in overseas countries were not counted under the policy if they do not obtain Chinese citizenship. Chinese citizens returning from abroad were allowed to have a second child. Sichuan province allowed exemptions for couples of certain backgrounds9.6% of Chinese couples were permitted two children regardless of their gender; and 1.6%—mainly Tibetans—had no limit at all.

Abolition of one-child policy

In October 2015, the Chinese news agency Xinhua announced plans of the government to abolish the one-child policy, now allowing all families to have two children (*Two-child policy*)

Failure in Implementation (Relaxation) of One-Child Policy in China

The following are some of them the reasons:

Twins sought:

Since there are no penalties for multiple births, it is believed that an increasing number of couples are turning to fertility medicines to induce the conception of twins.

"Four-two-one" problem:

As the first generation of law-enforced only-children came of age for becoming parents themselves, one adult child was left with having to provide support for his or her two parents and four grandparents. Called the "4-2-1 Problem", this leaves the older generations with increased chances of dependency on retirement funds or charity in order to receive support. If personal savings, pensions, or state welfare fails, most senior citizens would be left entirely dependent upon their very small family or neighbours for assistance.

If, for any reason, the single child is unable to care for their older adult relatives, the oldest generations would face a lack of resources and necessities. In response to such an issue, all provinces have decided that couples are allowed to have two children if both parents were only children themselves: By 2007, all provinces in the nation except Henan had adopted this new policy; Henan followed in 2011.

Unregistered children:

Heihaizior "black child" is a term applied in China. The term denotes children born outside the One-child policy, or generally children who are not registered in the Chinese national household registration system.

Being excluded from the family register (in effect, a birth certificate), they do not legally exist and as a result cannot access most public services, such as education and health care, and do not receive protection under the law.

Potential social problems:

Some parents may over-indulge their only child. The media referred to the indulged children in one-child families as "little emperors". Since the 1990s, some people have worried that this will result in a higher tendency toward poor social communication and cooperation skills amongst the new generation, as they have no siblings at home. No social studies have investigated the ratio of these over-indulged children and to what extent they are indulged. With the first generation of children born under the policy (which initially became a requirement for most couples with first children born starting in 1979 and extending into the 1980s) reaching adulthood, such worries were reduced.

However, the "little emperor syndrome" and additional expressions, describing the generation of Chinese singletons are very abundant in the Chinese media, Chinese academia and popular discussions. Being over-indulged, lacking self-discipline and having no adaptive capabilities are traits that are highly associated with Chinese singletons.

Birth tourism:

Chinese women gave birth to their second child overseas, a practice known as birth tourism. Many went to Hong Kong, which is exempt from the one-child policy. Likewise, a Hong Kong passport differs from China mainland passport by providing additional advantages. Recently though, the Hong Kong government has drastically reduced the quota of births set for non-local women in public hospitals. As a result, fees for delivering babies there have surged. As further admission cuts or a total ban on non-local births in Hong Kong are being considered, mainland agencies that arrange for expectant mothers to give birth overseas are predicting a surge in those going to North America.

As the United States practices birthright citizenship, children born in the US will be US citizens. The closest option (from China) is Saipan in the Northern

Mariana Islands, a US dependency in the western Pacific Ocean that allows Chinese visitors without visa restrictions. The island is currently experiencing an upswing in Chinese births. This option is used by relatively affluent Chinese who often have secondary motives as well, wishing their children to be able to leave mainland China when they grow older or bring their parents to the US.

Unequal enforcement:
Corrupted government officials and especially wealthy individuals have often been able to violate the policy in spite of fines.

Human rights violations:
The one-child policy has been challenged for violating a human right to determine the size of one's own family. According to a 1968 proclamation of the International Conference on Human Rights, Parents have a basic human right to determine freely and responsibly the number and the spacing of their children

The United Nations Population Fund's (UNFPA) support for family planning in China, which has been associated with the One-Child policy in the United States, led the United States Congress to pull out of the UNFPA during the Reagan administration, and again under George W. Bush's presidency, citing human rights abuses and stating that the right to "found a family" was protected under the Preamble in the Universal Declaration of Human Rights.

Effect on infanticide rates:
Sex-selected abortion, abandonment, and infanticide are illegal in China. Nevertheless, the US State Department, the Parliament of the United Kingdom, and the human rights organization Amnesty International have all declared that China's family planning programs contribute to infanticide. "The 'one-child' policy has also led to what first called 'Missing Women' or the 100 million girls 'missing' from the populations of China (and other developing countries) as a result of female infanticide, abandonment, and neglect".

Summary on the Policy of One Child in China
Reason for the establishment of one child policy in china:
1. High food shortage.
2. To reduce the high population grow that resulted by great leap forward.
3. To alleviate social, economic, and environmental problems.
4. A need of population that related to the national resources.
5. To reduce government expenses other burdens.

Implementation of one child policy

1. Provision of negative incentives (for those bare more than 1child) and positive incentives (for those bare one child as recommended) by the government
2. Throughout regular inspection
3. Introduction of family planning with forced birth control
4. Restriction and enforcement of laws so as to observe the policy.
5. Late marriage encouraged and early marriage discouraged.
6. Provision of education on the advantages of the policy.

Limitation of china one child policy:

1. Corruption to some government officers
2. Human right violation, hence china mate with obstacles in this policy
3. Lack of control in remote areas.
4. Resisted, because some where not willing to follow the policy implementation.
5. Birth tourism. Some Chinese arrange tour to other countries so as to have birth.
6. Hiding and confidentiality to the citizens. They did not report for those went against with the one child policy.

Impacts of one child policy in China:

1. Decline in birth rate.
2. Decline of population.
3. Led to gender imbalance.
4. Gender abuse, because women were mostly answerable.
5. Decline of work force.
6. Caused for ageing population.
7. Violation of child's right to live, because there were abortion by force if women found pregnant.

CASE STUDY: POPULATION POLICY OF TANZANIA

The population policy in Tanzania is revised policy of 1992, National population policy (NPP). Prior to 1992, Tanzania pursued implicit population policies and programmes. There some programmes were reflected in actions taken by the government in dealing with various issues, pertaining to population such as settlement schemes (1960's). Villagization programme (1970's) and programmes of implementation (1995). There were aspects like free social services; health, education as well as free supply of clean and safe water.

There were also programme of alleviation of illiteracy that were popularly called universal primary education. In 1992 it is when Tanzania adapted explicit population policy. *Therefore*; the government of Tanzania started the process of formulating the national population policy in 1986 and it was made in 1992. The country has a new population policy of 2006 that is in use to present (2016).

Major involvements and concerns of the national population policy: population and development planning issues; equality; equality; equity and social justice; natural resource and food production; information and databases and advocacy.

Goals and objectives of the Tanzania National Population Policy:
Objectives of the Tanzania National Population Policy include the followings:

1. To promote integrated rural-urban development;
2. To harmonize population and economic growth;
3. To promote gender, equity, equality and women empowerment;
4. To mobilize necessary resources for implementation of the National Population Policy;
5. To transform socio-economic and cultural values and attitudes that hinder gender equality;
6. To enhance the proper upbringing of children and youths;
7. To promote the well-being of the elderly and people with disabilities;
8. To promote the capacity of the country to address refugee problems;
9. To increase agricultural production;
10. To promote public awareness of individuals sexual and reproductive health and rights;
11. To promote and expand quality reproductive health care services;
12. To improve nutrition status of the people;

13. To promote employment opportunity;

14. To promote the integrated and sustainable use and management of natural resources;

15. To improve preparedness for and management of disasters and emergences;

16. To ensure an adequate supply of safe and clean water;

17. To promote and provide equitable and quality education;

18. To improve training in population issues;

19. To improve population data collection and research, and their timely dissemination and

20. To encourage the private sector, NGOs and religious organization to invest in the provision of education.

Guiding Principles for Implementation of National Population Policy

The implementation of population policy in Tanzania, guided by the following principles:

1. Recognition and appreciation of the central role of the government, Non-governmental organizations, private sectors, communities and individual in population and development,

2. Continued democratization of the political system with its attendant political pluralism as symbolized in the emergence of various political parties and the mushrooming of independent mass media,

3. Exploration of the country's non-renewable resources, taking into consideration the needs of future generations,

4. Consideration of regional and district variations with regard to the level of socio-economic development,

5. Adherence to the development vision, which among other things emphasizes the role of the market in determining resource allocation and use.

The Impacts of Population Policies to the Country (Positive Impacts)

The adopted National Population Policy in Tanzania was a revised document in 1992 by government which, the people of Tanzania resulted into the followings:

(1) Resettlement of the population in Tanzania.

(2) Village became more nucleated or mean nucleated in form.

(3) Provision of social services e.g. health services and education expanded.

(4) Establishment of clear network system from national level to the grassroots.

(5) Emergence of preliminary programmes of family planning services or maternal and child health (MCH)

(6) Taking the census after every 10 years is another good effect of National Population Policy (NPP).

Negative Impacts of Population Policy in Tanzania

(1) Loss of properties like farms, permanent crops during villagization process.

(2) In its implementation consumed a lot of money.

Problems or Limitations for Implementation of National Population Policy:

(1) Inadequate of human and financial resource.

(2) Non established and planned institutions.

(3) Inadequate recognition of the causal relationship between poverty, population, Environment, genders and development.

(4) Placing more emphasis on meeting demographic targets rather than the need of individuals male and female.

(5) The policies do implement foreign population policies.

Achievements of National Population Policy of 1992:

(a) Tanzania is now showing recognition of the links and interrelationship between population, resources and environmental development.

(b) Facilitated to the introduction and expansion of population studies in institutions of higher learning in the country.

(c) The policy facilitated the reduction of high population growth rate.

(d) Tanzania has improved in its status of contraceptive prevalence and the family planning involvement.

Test yourself:
1. Explain for the importance of population data in the government of Tanzania.
2. With vivid examples explain for importance of family planning and show why not Successful in Tanzania is by suggesting ways to curb such obstacles.
3. (a) Differentiate the implicit population policy from implicit population policy
   (b)What are the objectives of National population policy of 1992?
   (c)Describe the achievement of the National population policy of Tanzania.
4. National population policy of1992 failed on its implementation. Justify

CHAPTER 16:

POPULATION STRUCTURE

By definition; population structure is analyzed in terms of age and sex grouping and is represented by population pyramids. Population pyramid have two bar graphs; one for males and one for females. The structures can give information about the following:

- *Life Expectancy:* is how long on average people can expect to live
- *Infant Mortality*: is the number of babies who die under the age of 5 years per 1000 people
- *Economically Active:* are people in work between the ages 16-65
- Young Dependents: are children under 15 years old who are dependent on the economically active people for their needs.
- *Elderly Dependents:* are people usually over 60 who are dependent on the younger economically active people.

By studying such diagrams (pyramids) it is possible to gain a clear idea of the population characteristics of any given country. The following are definitions of the main population *terms* used in such analysis:

1. **Birth rate**: is the number of live births per 1, 000 of the population.
2. **Death rate:** is the number of deaths per 1, 000 of the population.
3. **Infant mortality rate:** is the number of deaths of children below 1 year of age per 1, 000 of the population.
4. **Life expectancy:** is the average age at which people die.
5. **Natural increase:** is the excess of births over deaths per 1, 000 of population. This does not include increase in population due to immigration.
6. **Net reproduction ratio**: is the rate at which women are replaced by daughters who will have children. More boys are born than girls. This is

natural way of keeping population even for mortality is higher among men.

Characteristics of Population Structure

Population structure has the following characteristics:

1. Exponential in growth, e.g. 2, 4, 16, 32, etc.
2. Have age sex structure.
3. It is unevenly distributed.
4. It is dynamic.
5. Differ in level of technology and development.
6. Faces different problems.

Importance of Population Structure

Population structure is important in the following ways:

1. Demographic projection.
2. Provision of social services.
3. Determination of social role and status.
4. Population policy formulation.
5. Government planning.
6. Determining the future labor forces.
7. Population control.
8. Serving and helping the marginalized groups.

POPULATION PYRAMID

Population pyramid also called as *age-sex pyramid*, *age pyramid* or *age picture diagram*. Population pyramid is a graphical illustration that shows the distribution of various age groups in a population (typically that of a country or region of the world), which forms the shape of a pyramid when the population is growing. It is also used in ecology to determine the overall age distribution of a population; an indication of the reproductive capabilities and likelihood of the continuation of a species.

It typically consists of two back-to-back bar graphs, with the population plotted on the X-axis and age on the Y-axis, one showing the number of males and one showing females in a particular population in five-year age groups (also called cohorts). Males are conventionally shown on the left and females on the right, and they may be measured by raw number or as a percentage of the total population.

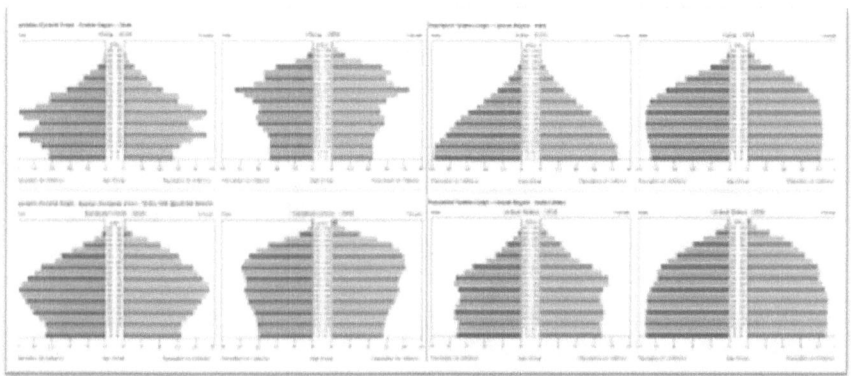

Population pyramids are often viewed as the most effective way to graphically depict the age and sex distribution of a population, partly because of the very clear image these pyramids present.

A great deal of information about the population broken down by age and sex can be read from a population pyramid, and this can shed light on the extent of development and other aspects of the population. A population pyramid also tells how many people of each age range live in the area. There tends to be more females than males in the older age groups, due to females' longer life expectancy.

Characteristics of Population Pyramid

Population pyramid has the following characteristics as namely below:

1. Shows ages structure of the population.
2. Shows sex structure of the population.
3. Shows the level of development of any country.
4. Shows the level of technology in the country.
5. Shows the relationship between working group and dependent group.

Presentation of Age Sex Structure

Population age sex structure is presented into population pyramid.

Shape and Stages of Population Pyramid

There are different shapes to the pyramids which tell us different things about the population of the country. It is often useful to divide population pyramids into 3 distinct age groups or *Cohorts* (0-15 the Young), 16-65 (the working age) and 65 and above (as the retired sectors of the population). Knowing the percentage of people in these sectors can allow us to calculate a Dependency Ratio.

This is the ratio between those of working age and those of non-working age. The no-working age are known as *dependents* because they depend upon the working age people to provide for their needs. This is calculated as:

$$\frac{\% \text{ pop aged } 0 - 14 + \% \text{ pop aged } 65+}{\% \text{ of population aged } 15-65} \times 100$$

The ratio for an MEDC (Most Economic Developed Countries) usually lies between 0.5 and 0.75. The ratio for an LEDC (Least Developed Countries) is typically higher. Mexico, with a youthful population structure, has a dependency ratio of 1.04. (CIA Fact book).

Stage 1— High Fluctuating Population Pyramid.

A population pyramid typical of stage 1, have a wide base, low life expectancy and concave profile. This stage one of population pyramid represents LDCs (Least Developed Countries) that are High Fluctuating These countries have a concave profile because they have high birth rates and high death rates, plus low life expectancies.

Very few people survive to old age (the average life and birth rates are very high. This cause the population at the base to be prominent and grow through momentum every year, but these groups are compensated by Stage 2 that are rapid growing.

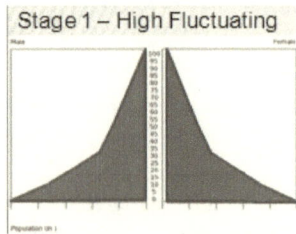

Stage 2 – Early Expanding Population Pyramid

A population pyramid typical of stage 2, note the wide base, lengthening life expectancy and pyramidal profile. This stage has a triangular shaped pyramid.

The stage of pyramid describes LEDCs (Rapidly Growing countries). Pyramids found in this stage, they have lots of children and people do not tend to live for a long time (low Life expectancy). These countries populations grow rapidly as many more children are added to the population than people die. This does not sound like a big percentage. The Demographic Transition Model has high dependency.

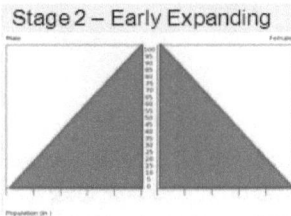

Stage 3 – Late Expanding Population Pyramid
A population pyramid of stage 3 has narrowing base, increasing life expectancy and rocket shaped profile.

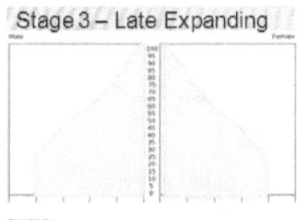

Stage 4 – Low Fluctuation Population Pyramid
A population pyramid typical of stage 4 have the narrowing base, long life expectancy and vase shaped profile. This stage of population pyramid represents MEDCs with stable population. Most MEDCs have a space rocket shape, with old people living for a long time (high life expectancy), lots of workers and reasonable numbers of children. These populations are stable and are growing slowly as the number of young is just above the number of people dying.

Some MEDCs actually have declining populations where there are not enough children being born each year to replace those dying. Germany is experiencing a period of negative growth (-0.1%). As negative growth in a country continues, the population is reduced. A population can shrink due to a low birth rate and a stable death rate. Increased emigration may also be a contributor to a declining population.

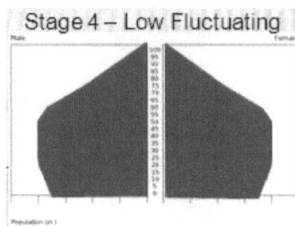

Stage 5 – Contracting/Declining Population Pyramid

A population pyramid typical of stage 5 note the ever diminishing base and very long life expectancies.

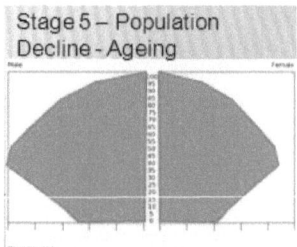

Generally; the five stages of population pyramid can be presented in a sequence as shown in the following diagram:

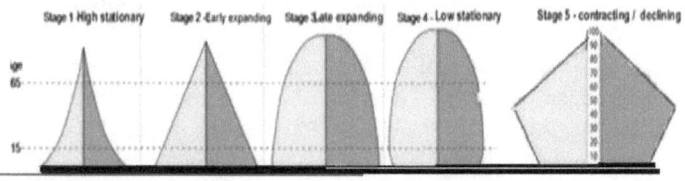

Types of Population Pyramid (Model of Age Sex Structure)

While all countries' population pyramids differ, three general types population have been identified by the fertility and mortality rates of a country. Below are the three types of population pyramids: expansive, constrictive, and stationary:

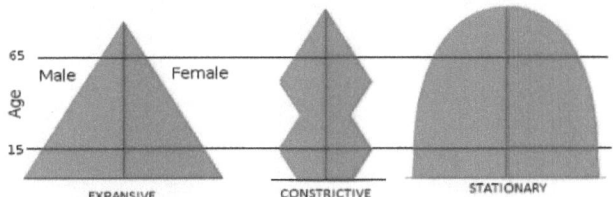

Stationary pyramid:

Stationary population pyramids are those that show a somewhat equal proportion of the population in each age group. There is not a decrease or increase in population: it is stable. Austria has a stationary population pyramid.

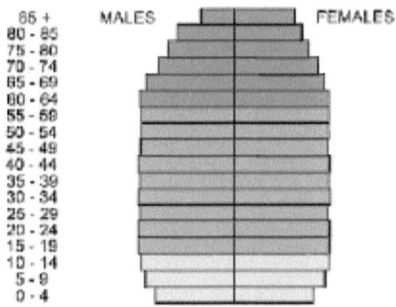

The countries represented these types of population pyramids indicates low fertility and low mortality, very similar to a constrictive pyramid.

Expansive (progressive) pyramid:

A population pyramid that is very wide at the base, indicating high birth and death rates. Expansive population pyramids depict populations that have a larger percentage of people in younger age groups. Populations with this shape usually have high fertility rates with lower life expectancies. Many third world countries have expansive population pyramids

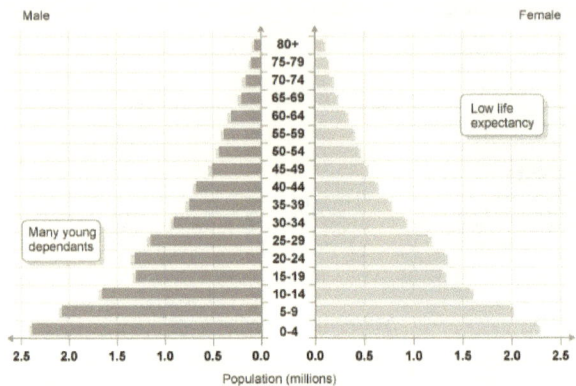

Constrictive (regressive) pyramid:

It is a population pyramid that comes in at the bottom. The population is generally older on average, as the country has long life expectancy, a low death rate, but also a low birth rate. This pyramid is becoming more common, especially when immigrants are factored out, and is a typical pattern for a very developed country, a high level of education, easy access to and incentive to use birth control, good health care, and few negative environmental factors.

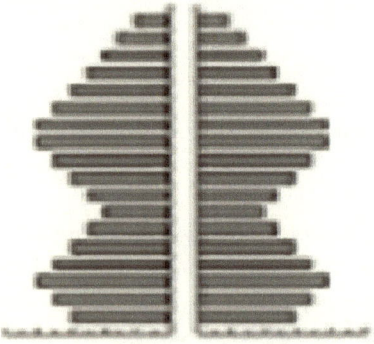

NOTE: In some countries the above "pyramids" are referred to by a description of their shape. The stationary pyramid is referred to as a "clock-model" (like the bell in a clock tower). The contracting pyramid is referred to as "onion" shaped. Sometimes even as "urn" shaped.

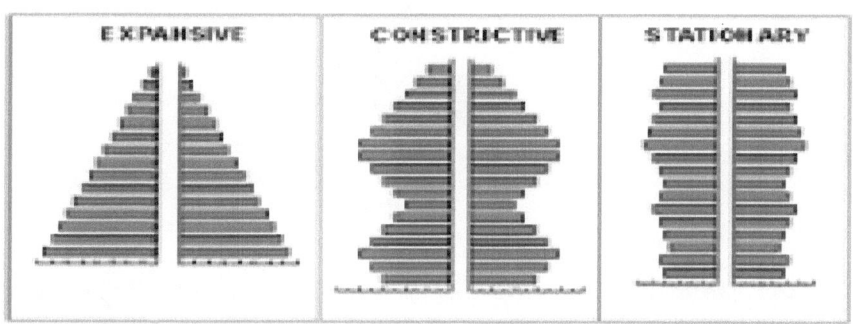

Population Pyramid and Levels of the Country's Development:

The structure of population pyramids tends to determine the level of development of the particular country:

(I) Population Pyramid for Least Developing Countries: Main Features of an LEDC - e.g. Ethiopia, Tanzania and Bangladesh:

- The wide base indicates a high proportion of children.
- Large families reflect the low status of women, early marriages, lack of education and little family planning available.
- The steep sides show that the death rate is high for both the young and adults.
- Life expectancy is also low with few people reaching old age
- High death rates reflect the lack of medication, clean water and regular food supplies.
- Populations are growing rapidly and in the case of Nigeria are expected to double in 25 years.

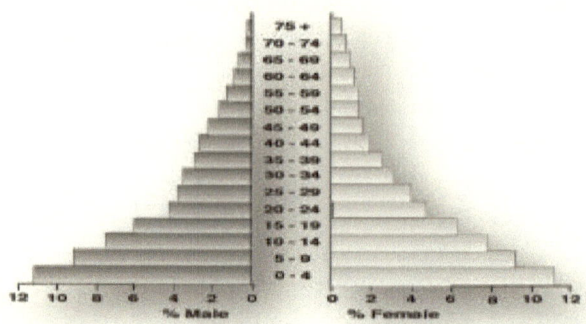

<u>**Qn**</u>: *State for the Characteristics of the pyramid for least developing countries (6 points).*

(II) Population Pyramid for Developed Countries: Main Features of an MEDC - e.g. Britain, Germany and USA:

- Narrow base with many women having less than two children.
- Women are marrying later.
- Contraception is universal in countries such as Britain.
- Excellent medical care and high standards of living mean the infant death rate is low - most children live to middle and old age.
- Death rates are low and are only high in extreme old age which gives the pyramid its straight sides.
- On average women can expect to live to 83 years and men to 76 years.

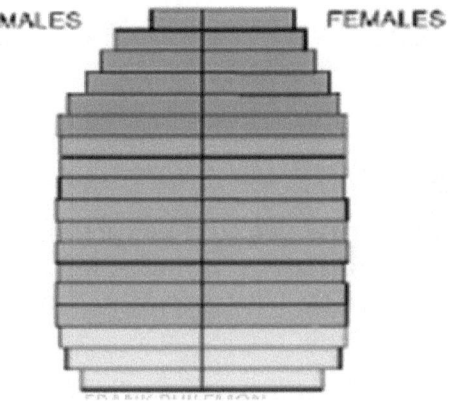

<u>Qn</u>: State for the Characteristics of the pyramid for developed countries (7 points).

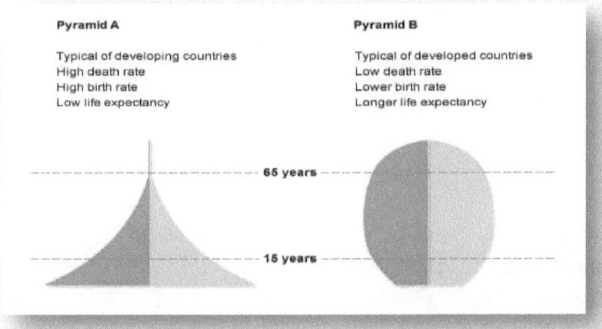

Uses of Population Pyramids

Population pyramids can be used to find the number of economic dependents being supported in a particular population. Economic dependents are defined as those under 15 (children who are in full-time education and therefore unable to work) and those over 65 (those who have the option of being retired). In some less developed countries children start work well before the age of 15, and in some developed countries it is common to not start work until 30 (like in the North European countries), and people may work beyond the age of 65, or retire early.

Therefore, the definition provides an approximation. In many countries, the government plans the economy in such a way that the working population can support these dependents. This number can be further used to calculate the dependency ratio in that population. Population pyramids can be used to observe the natural increase, birth, and death rate.

POPULATION STRUCTURE OF NORWAY

Norway is the 61st largest country in the world. In 2013, the population in Norway was 5.1 million people. Life expectancy in Norway estimated as 78.9 years for male, and 83.2 years for female.

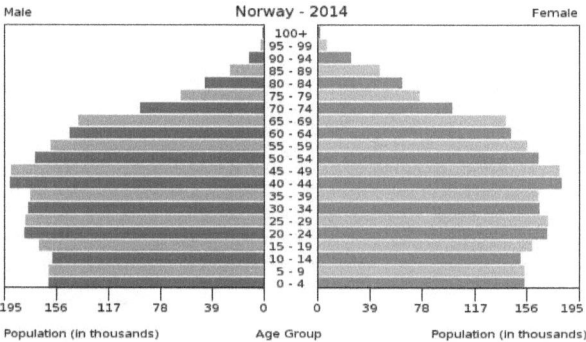

In the last decades, Norway has become home to increasing numbers of immigrants, foreign workers, and asylum-seekers from various parts of the world. Norway had a steady influx of immigrants from South Asia (mostly Pakistanis and Sri Lankans), East Asia (mainly the Chinese), and SoutheastAsia (e.g. Filipinos), EasternEurope (e.g. Russians and Poles),Sou thern Europe (Greeks, Albanians and people from former Yugoslavia etc.), and West Asian countries (especially Iraqis and Palestinians), as well as Somalis, Turks, Moroccans, and some Latin Americans.

After ten Eastern European and Baltic countries joined the EU in 2004, there has also been a substantial influx of people from Poland, Estonia, Latvia and Lithuania. As of 2012, an official study shows that 86.2% of the total population has at least one parent who is born in Norway and more than 660 000 individuals (13.2%) are migrants and their descendants; numbering 110 000 second generation migrants born in Norway. Of these 660 000 immigrants and their descendants:

- 335 000 (51%) have a Western background (Australia, North America, elsewhere in Europe)
- 325 000 (49%) have a non-Western background (Morocco, Iraq, Somalia, Pakistan, Iran).

In 2012, of the total 660 000 with immigrant background, 407,262 had Norwegian citizenship (62.2 percent).

Immigrants were represented in all Norwegian municipalities. The cities or municipalities with the highest share of immigrants in 2012 were Oslo (26 percent) and Drammen (18 percent). The share in Stavanger was 16%.According to Reuters, Oslo is the "fastest growing city in Europe because of increased immigration". In recent years, immigration has accounted for most of Norway's population growth. In 2011 16% of newborn children were of immigrant background.

As of 2012, an official study shows that the quotient of the total population that is either born outside Norway, or has one or two parents born abroad, or has one or more grandparents born abroad is 1 100 000 to 5 017 500 (which equals 21.9 percent).

About a half million of these, however, identify as ethnic Norwegians who may have, for example, one Swedish grandparent. As of 2012, an official study shows that 86.2% of the total population are ethnic Norwegians and more than 660 000 individuals (13.2%) are migrants and their descendants (110 000 second generation migrants born in Norway). Of these 660 000 immigrants and their descendants: 335 000 (51%) have a Western background (Australia, North America, Europe). 325 000 (49%) have a non-Western background (Turkey, Morocco, Iraq, Somalia, Pakistan, Iran

Historical Age Structure

1860 estimation: *0–14 years:* 35.9% (male 288,510; female 280,249) *15–64 years:* 58.0% (male 446,391; female 472,405) *65 years and over:* 6.1% (male 42,130; female 53,840)

1910 estimation: *0–14 years:* 35.0% (male 423,253; female 408,204) *15–64 years:* 57.3% (male 640,835; female 722,443) *65 years and over:* 7.7% (male 82,312; female 99,905)

1960 estimation: *0–14 years:* 26.0% (male 476,748; female 452,559) *15–64 years:* 63.0% (male 1,125,525; female 1,123,206) *65 years and over:* 11.0% (male 175,485; female 214,184)

2010 estimation: *0–14 years:* 18.9% (male 470,253; female 447,472) *15–64 years:* 66.2% (male 1,641,821; female 1,575,980) *65 years and over:* 14.9% (male 314,678; female 407,995)

2060 estimation: *0–14 years:* 17.4% (male 628,729; female 596,683) *15–64 years:* 58.7% (male 2,114,792; female 2,016,030) *65 years and over:* 23.9% (male 805,111; female 871,342

Median Age

2010 estimation: *total:* 39.7 years, *male:* 38.8 years, *female:* 40.5 years

Urbanization

2011estimation: *urban population:* 79.2% of total population

2005-10 estimation: *Rate of urbanization:* 0.7% annual rate of change

Sex Ratio

2004 estimation: *at birth:* 1.05 male(s)/female, *under 15 years:* 1.05 male(s)/female' *15–64 years:* 1.04 male(s)/female *65 years and over:* 0.72 male(s)/female, *total population:* 0.98 male(s)/female

Infant Mortality Rate
2005 estimation: *total:* 3.1 deaths/1,000 live births, *male:* 3.3 deaths/1,000 live births, *female:* 2.9 deaths/1,000 live births

Life Expectancy at Birth
2010 estimation: *total population:* 81.04 years, *male:* 78.85 years, *female:* 83.15 years.

POPULATION STRUCTURE IN CHINA
China is the 3rd largest country in the world after USSR and Canada. China is estimated to have 1.394 billion total populations in 2015. The population density is 145 people per km^2. 54% is in urban by 2014.

The demographics of the People's Republic of China are identified by a large population with a relatively small youth division, which is partially a result of China's one-child policy. Chinese population reached the billion mark in 1982. China's population is over 1.355 billion, the largest of any country in the world. According to the 2010 census, 91.51% of the population was Han Chinese, and 8.49% were minorities. China's population growth rate is only 0.47%, ranking 159th in the world. China conducted its sixth national population census on 1 November 2010.

Historical population of China (Source: Census of China)		
Census	**Population.**	**Percentage**
1953	582,603,417	
1964	694,581,759	19.2%
1982	1,008,175,288	45.1%

1990	1,133,682,501	12.4%
2000	1,265,830,000	11.7%
2010	1,339,724,852	5.8%

Birth rate in China

Initially, China's post-1949 leaders were ideologically disposed to view a large population as an asset. But the liabilities of a large, rapidly growing population soon became apparent. For one year, starting in August 1956, vigorous support was given to the Ministry of Public Health's mass birth control efforts. These efforts, however, had little impact on fertility. After the interval of the Great Leap Forward, Chinese leaders again saw rapid population growth as an obstacle to development, and their interest in birth control revived.

In the early 1960s, schemes somewhat more muted than during the first campaign, emphasized the virtues of late marriage. Birth control offices were set up in the central government and some provincial-level governments in 1964. The second campaign was particularly successful in the cities, where the birth rate was cut in half during the 1963–66 periods. The upheaval of the Cultural Revolution brought the program to a halt, however.

In 1972 and 1973 the party mobilized its resources for a nationwide birth control campaign administered by a group in the State Council. Committees to oversee birth control activities were established at all administrative levels and in various collective enterprises. This extensive and seemingly effective network covered both the rural and the urban population. In urban areas public security headquarters included population control sections. In rural areas the country's "barefoot doctors" distributed information and contraceptives to people's commune members.

By 1973 Mao Zedong was personally identified with the family planning movement, signifying a greater leadership commitment to controlled population growth than ever before. Yet until several years after Mao's death in 1976, the leadership was reluctant to put forth directly the rationale that population control was necessary for economic growth and improved living standards.

Population growth targets were set for both administrative units and individual families. In the mid-1970s the maximum recommended family size was two children in cities and three or four in the country. Since 1979 the government has advocated a one-child limit for both rural and urban areas and has generally set a maximum of two children in special circumstances. As of 1986 the policy for minority nationalities was two children per couple, three in special circumstances, and no limit for ethnic groups with very small populations. The overall goal of the one-child policy was to keep the total population within 1.2 billion through the year 2000.

The one-child policy was a highly ambitious population control program. Like previous programs of the 1960s and 1970s, the one-child policy employed a combination of public education, social pressure, and in some cases coercion. The one-child policy was unique, however, in that it linked reproduction with economic cost or benefit.

Under the one-child program, a sophisticated system rewarded those who observed the policy and penalized those who did not. Couples with only one child were given a "one-child certificate" entitling them to such benefits as cash bonuses, longer maternity leave, better child care, and preferential housing assignments. In return, they were required to pledge that they would not have more children. In the countryside, there was great pressure to adhere to the one-child limit. Because the rural population accounted for approximately 60% of the total, the effectiveness of the one-child policy in rural areas was considered the key to the success or failure of the program as a whole.

In rural areas the day-to-day work of family planning was done by cadres at the team and brigade levels who were responsible for women's affairs and by health workers. The women's team leader made regular household visits to keep track of the status of each family under her jurisdiction and collected information on which women were using contraceptives, the methods used, and which had become pregnant. She then reported to the brigade women's leader, who documented the information and took it to a monthly meeting of the commune birth-planning committee.

According to reports, ceilings or quotas had to be adhered to; to satisfy these cutoffs, unmarried young people were persuaded to postpone marriage, couples without children were advised to "wait their turn," women with unauthorized pregnancies were pressured to have abortions, and those who already had children were urged to use contraception or undergo sterilization. Couples with more than one child were exhorted to be sterilized.

The one-child policy enjoyed much greater success in urban than in rural areas. Even without state intervention, there were compelling reasons for urban couples to limit the family to a single child. Raising a child required a significant portion of family income, and in the cities a child did not become an economic asset until he or she entered the work force at age sixteen. Couples with only one child were given preferential treatment in housing allocation. In addition, because city dwellers who were employed in state enterprises received pensions after retirement, the sex of their first child was less important to them than it was to those in rural areas.

Observers suggested that an accurate assessment of the one-child program would not be possible until all women who came of childbearing age in the early 1980s passed their fertile years. As of 1987 the one-child program had achieved mixed results. In general, it was very successful in almost all urban areas but less successful in rural areas.

Rapid fertility reduction associated with the one-child policy has potentially negative results. For instance, in the future the elderly might not be able to rely on their children to care for them as they have in the past, leaving the state to assume the expense, which could be considerable. Based on United Nations and Chinese government statistics, it was estimated in 1987 that by the year 2000 the population 60 years and older (the retirement age is 60 in urban areas) would number 127 million, or 10.1% of the total population; the projection for 2025 was 234 million elderly, or 16.4%.

According to projections based on the 1982 census, if the one-child policy were maintained to the year 2000, 25% of China's population would be age 65 or older by the year 2040. Currently, at the end of 2015, the government of have allowed two children birth per family.

Population Density and Distribution in China

China is the most populated country in the world and its national population density (137/km^2) is similar to those of Switzerland and the Czech Republic. The overall population density of China conceals major regional variations, the western and northern part have a few million people, while eastern half has about 1.3 billion. The vast majority of China's population lives near the east in major cities.

Coast and Eastern China

In the 11 provinces, special municipalities, and autonomous regions along the southeast coast, population density was 320.6 people per km². Broadly speaking, the population was concentrated east of the mountains and south of the northern steppe. The most densely populated areas included the Yangtze River Valley (of which the delta region was the most populous), Sichuan Basin, North China Plain, Pearl River Delta, and the industrial area around the city of Shenyang in the northeast.

Western Areas

Population is most sparse in the mountainous, desert, and grassland regions of the northwest and southwest. In Inner Mongolia Autonomous Region, portions are completely uninhabited, and only a few sections have populations denser than ten people per km². The Inner Mongolia, Xinjiang, and Tibet autonomous regions and Qinghai and Gansu comprise 55% of the country's land area but in 1985 contained only 5.7% of its population.

Gender Disparity Concern

Future challenges for China will be the gender disparity. According to the 2010 census, males account for 51.27% of China's 1.34 billion people, while females made up 48.73% of the total. The sex ratio (the number of males for each female in a population) at birth was 118.06 boys to every 100 girls (54.14%) in 2010, higher than the 116.86 (53.89%) of 2000, but 0.53 points lower than the ratio of 118.59 (54.25%) in 2005. In most western countries the sex ratio at birth is around 105 boys to 100 girls (51.22%). At the moment there are about 9 million more boys than girls in China.

Population Projection

US Census Bureau, 2010 estimation: In 1949 crude death rates were probably higher than 30 per 1,000, and the average life expectancy was only 35 years. Beginning in the early 1950s, mortality steadily declined; it continued to decline through 1978 and remained relatively constant through 1987. One major fluctuation was reported in a computer reconstruction of China's population trends from 1953 to 1987 produced by the United States Bureau of the Census. The computer model showed that the crude death rate increased dramatically during the famine years associated with the Great Leap Forward (1958–60).

According to Chinese government statistics, the crude birth rate followed five distinct patterns from 1949 to 1982. It remained stable from 1949 to 1954, varied widely from 1955 to 1965, experienced fluctuations between 1966 and 1969, dropped sharply in the late 1970s, and increased from 1980 to 1981. Between 1970 and 1980, the crude birth rate dropped from 33.4 per 1,000 to 18.2 per 1,000. The government attributed this dramatic decline in fertility to the *wǎn xī shǎo*, or "late, long, few": later marriages, longer intervals between births, and fewer children) birth control campaign.

However, elements of socioeconomic change, such as increased employment of women in both urban and rural areas and reduced infant mortality (a greater percentage of surviving children would tend to reduce demand for additional children), may have played some role. The birth rate increased in the 1980s to a level over 20 per 1,000, primarily as a result of a marked rise in marriages and first births. The rise was an indication of problems with the one-child policy of 1979. Chinese sources, however, indicate that the birth rate started to decrease again in the 1990s and reached a level of around 12 per 1,000 in recent years.

In urban areas, the housing shortage may have been at least partly responsible for the decreased birth rate. Also, the policy in force during most of the 1960s and the early 1970s of sending large numbers of high school graduates to the countryside deprived cities of a significant proportion of persons of childbearing age and undoubtedly had some effect on birth rates (see Cultural Revolution (1966–76)). Primarily for economic reasons, rural birth rates tended to decline less than urban rates.

The right to grow and sell agricultural products for personal profit and the lack of an old-age Welfare system were incentives for rural people to produce many children, especially sons, for help in the fields and for support in old age. Because of these conditions, it is unclear to what degree education had been able to erode traditional values favoring large families.

Today, the population continues to grow. There is also a serious gender imbalance. Census data obtained in 2000 revealed that 119 boys were born for every 100 girls, and among China's "floating population" the ratio was as high as 128:100. These situations led the government in July 2004 to ban selective abortions of female fetuses. It is estimated that this imbalance will rise until 2025–2030 to reach 20% then slowly decrease.

China now has an increasingly aging population; it is projected that 11.8% of the population in 2020 will be 65 years of age and older. Health care has improved dramatically in China since 1949. Major diseases such as cholera, typhoid, and scarlet fever have been brought under control. Life expectancy has more than doubled, and infant mortality has dropped significantly.

On the negative side, the incidence of cancer, cerebrovascular disease, and heart disease has increased to the extent that these have become the leading causes of death. Economic reforms initiated in the late 1970s fundamentally altered methods of providing health care; the collective medical care system has been gradually replaced by a more individual-oriented approach.

In Hong Kong, the birth rate of 0.9% is lower than its death rate. Hong Kong's population increases because of immigration from the mainland and a large expatriate population comprising about 4%. Like Hong Kong, Macau also has a low birth rate relying on immigration to maintain its population.

Total Fertility Rate

According to the 2000 census, the TFR (Total Fertility Rate) was 1.22 (0.86 for cities, 1.08 for towns and 1.43 for villages/outposts). Beijing had the lowest TFR at 0.67, while Guizhouhad the highest at 2.19. The Xiangyang district of Jiamusi city (Heilongjiang) has a TFR of 0.41, which is the lowest TFR recorded anywhere in the world in recorded history. Other extremely low TFR counties are: 0.43 in the Heping district of Tianjin city (Tianjin), and 0.46 in the Mawei district of Fuzhou city (Fujian). At the other end TFR was 3.96 in Geji County (Tibet), 4.07 in Jiali County (Tibet), and 5.47 in Baqing County (Tibet).

The 2010 census reported a TFR of 1.18 (0.88 in cities, 1.15 in townships, and 1.44 in rural areas). The five regions with the lowest fertility rates were Beijing (0.71), Shanghai (0.74), Liaoning (0.74), Heilongjiang (0.75), and Jilin (0.76). The five regions with the highest fertility rates were Guangxi (1.79), Guizhou (1.75),Xinjiang (1.53), Hainan (1.51), and Anhui (1.48).

Total fertility rate by ethnic group (2010census): Han (1.14), Zhuang (1.59), Hui (1.48), Manchu (1.18), Uyghur (2.04), Miao (1.82), Yi (1.82), Tujia (1.74), Tibetan (1.60), Mongols (1.26).

Labor Force

In 2012, for the first time, according to statistics released by China's National Bureau of Statistics in January 2013, the number of people theoretically able to enter the Chinese labor force (individuals aged 15 to 59), shrank slightly to 937.27 million people, a decrease of 3.45 million from 2011. This trend, resulting from China's demographic transition, is anticipated to continue for at least the next 20 years, to 2030. The CIA World Fact Book estimates the actual active labor force to amount to 798.5 million.

Height and Weight

As of 2012, the average Chinese man was 167.1 centimeters tall (5 ft 5.8 in) in 2012, the figures showed, and women's average height was 155.8 centimeters (5 ft 1.3 in). The same study showed an average Chinese man weighed 66.2 kilograms (145.9 lbs, or 10 stone 5.9 lbs), up 3.5 kilograms (7.7 lbs) over 10 years, while women were 2.9 kilograms (6.4 pounds) heavier on average at 57.3 kilograms (126.3 pounds, or 9 stone 0.3 lbs). They were up just 0.4 centimeters (0.16 in) and 0.7 centimeters (0.28 in) respectively from 10 years earlier.

Ethnic Groups

The People's Republic of China (PRC) officially recognizes 56 distinct ethnic groups, the largest of which are Han, who constitute 91.51% of the total population in 2010. Ethnic minorities constitute 8.49% or 113.8 million of China's population in 2010. During the past decades ethnic minorities have experienced higher growth rates than the majority Han population, because they are not under the one-child policy.

Their proportion of the population in China has grown from 6.1% in 1953, to 8.04% in 1990, 8.41% in 2000 and 8.49% in 2010. Large ethnic minorities (data according to the 2000 census) include the Zhuang (16 million, 1.28%), Manchu (10 million,0.84%), Uyghur (9 million,0.78%), Hui (9 million, 0.71%), Miao (8 million,0.71%), Yi (7 million,0.61%), Tujia (5.75 million,0.63 %), Mongols (5 million,0.46%), Tibetan (5 million, 0.43%), Buyi (3 million, 0.23%), and Korean (2 million, 0.15%).

People from Other Immigration Jurisdictions

The 2010 Census counted 234,829 residents from Hong Kong, 21,201 residents from Macao, 170,283 residents from Taiwan, and 593,832 residents from other locations, totaling 1,020,145 residents

Migration

Internal migration in the People's Republic of China is one of the most extensive in the world according to the International Labor Organization. In fact, research done by Kam Wing Chan of the University of

Washington suggests that "In the 30 years since 1979, China's urban population has grown by about 440 million to 622 million in 2009. Of the 440 million increases, about 340 million was attributable to net migration and urban reclassification.

Even if only half of that increase was migration, the volume of rural-urban migration in such a short period is likely the largest in human history." Migrants in China are commonly members of floating, which refers primarily to migrants in China without local household registration status through the Chinese Hukou system. In general, rural-urban migrant workers are most excluded from local educational resources, city-wide social welfare programs and many jobs because of their lack of hukou status.

In 2011 a total of 252.78 million migrant workers (an increase of 4.4% compared to 2010) existed in China. Out of these, migrant workers who left their hometown and worked in other provinces accounted for 158.63 million (an increase of 3.4% compared to 2010) and migrant workers who worked within their home provinces reached 94.15 million (an increase of 5.9% compared to 2010). Estimations are that Chinese cities will face an influx of another 243 million migrants by 2025, taking the urban population up to nearly 1 billion people.

This population of migrants would represent "almost 40 percent of the total urban population," a number which is almost three times the current level. While it is often difficult to collect accurate statistical data on migrant floating populations, the number of migrants is undoubtedly quite large. "In China's largest cities, for instance, it is often quoted that at least one out of every five persons is a migrant."

China's government influences the pattern of urbanization through the Hukou permanent residence registration system, land-sale policies, infrastructure investment and the incentives offered to local government officials. The other factors influencing migration of people from rural provincial areas to large cities are employment, education, business opportunities and higher standard of living.

The mass emigration known as the Chinese Diaspora, which occurred from the 19th century to 1949, was mainly caused by wars and starvation in mainland China, invasion from various foreign countries, as well as the problems resulting from political corruption. Most immigrants were illiterate peasants and manual laborers, called "coolies" by analogy to the same pattern of immigration from India, who emigrated to work in countries such as the Americas, Australia, South Africa and Southeast Asia.

Urbanization

Urbanization increased in speed following the initiation of the reform and opening policy. By the end of 2014, 54.7% of the total population lived in urban areas, a rate that rose from 26% in 1990.

The following demographic statistics are from the CIA World Fact book. No statistics have been included for areas currently governed by the Republic of China (Taiwan). Unless stated otherwise, statistics refer only to mainland. (See Demographics of Hong Kong and Demographics of Macau.)

Population:

- *Mainland only: 1,338,612,968 (2009)*
- *Hong Kong: 7,055,071 (2009)*
- *Macau: 559,846 (2009)*
- *Total: 1,346,227,885 (2009).*

Urban-rural ratio:

- *Urban: 49.68% (2010) — 665,570,000*
- *Rural: 50.32% (2010) — 674,150,000*

Age structure:

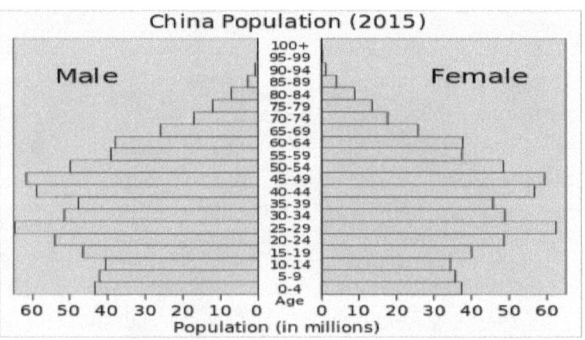

- *0–14 years: 16.60% (2011)*

- *15–64 years: 72.1% (male 495,724,889/female 469,182,087) (2009)*

Population growth rate:

- *Population growth rate: 0.57% (2000–2010 average)*

Sex distribution:

- *Sex distribution: male 51.27%; female 48.73% (2010)*

Sex ratio (Source: National Bureau of Statist in China):

- *At birth: 1.133 male(s)/female (2011)*
- *Under 15 years: 1.17 male(s)/female (2011)*
- *15–64 years: 1.06 male(s)/female (2011)*
- *65 years and over: 0.93 male(s)/female (2011)*
- *Total population: 1.06 male(s)/female (2011)*

Infant mortality rate:

- *Total: 15.2 deaths/1,000 live births (2013 estimtion)*
- *Male: 15.16 deaths/1,000 live births (2013 estimation)*
- *Female: 15.25 deaths/1,000 live births (2013 estimation)*

Child mortality:

- *415,000 children (under 16) died in China in 2006 (4.3% of the world total)*

Life expectancy at birth:

- *Total population: 74.99 years (2013)*
- *Male: 72.96 years (2013)*
- *Female: 77.27 years (2013)*

Marriage and divorce:

- *Marriage rate: 6.3/1,000 population (2006)*
- *Divorce rate: 1.0/1,000 population (2006)*

Literacy rate (Age 15 and over can read and write):

- *Total population: 95.92% (2010 census)*
- *Male: 95.1% (2000 census)*
- *Female: 86.5% (2000 census)*

Educational attainment (As of 2000, percentage of population age 15 and over having):

- *no schooling and incomplete primary: 15.6%*
- *completed primary: 35.7%*
- *some secondary: 34.0%*
- *complete secondary: 11.1%*
- *some postsecondary through advanced degree: 3.6%*

Religious affiliation (Main article: Religion in China):

- *Predominantly: Mahayana Buddhism, Taoism (Chinese-folk-religion), Confucianism (via ancestral worship).*
- *Others: Christianity (3% – 4%), Islam (1.5%), ethnic minority religions, others.*
- *Note: State atheism, but traditionally pragmatic and eclectic.*

POPULATION STRUCTURE IN TANZANIA

Tanzania has total area of 94, 500km^2. The total population in Tanzania was last recorded at 47.4 million people in 2014 from 10.1 million in 1960, changing 371 percent during the last 50 years. Population in Tanzania averaged 25.04 Million from 1960 until 2014, reaching an all-time high of 47.42 Million in 2014 and a record low of 10.07 Million in 1960. Population in Tanzania is reported by the National Bureau of Statistics, Tanzania. In 2015, the population of Tanzania is estimated to 49.25 million.

Most of the population in Tanzania is found in urban areas and areas with good climatic conditions, water, and fertile soils. More than 70% of the people in

Tanzania are living in rural areas; where are engaging in animal keeping and crop cultivation.

According to the 2012 census, the total population was 44,928,923 compared to 12,313,469 in 1967, resulting in an annual growth rate of 2.9 percent. The under 15 age group represented 44.1 percent of the population, with 35.5 percent being in the 15–35 age group, 52.2 percent being in the 15–64 age group, and 3.8 percent being older than 64.

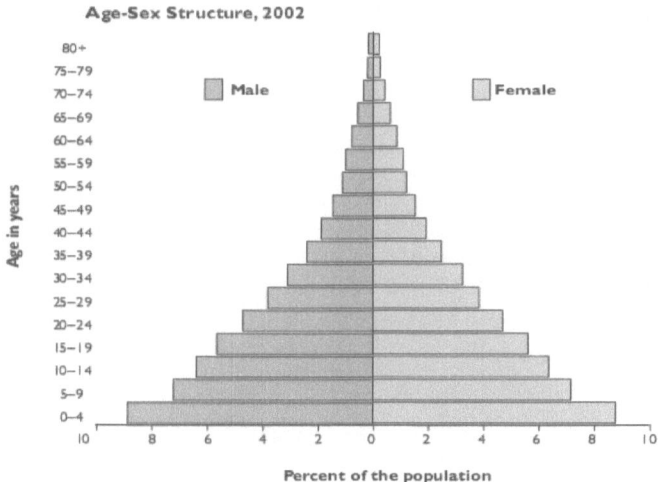

Population pyramid of Tanzania: source *2002 population housing and census*

According to the 2012 revision of the World Population Prospects, children below the age of 15 constituted 44.8 percent of the total population, with 52.0 percent aged 15–64 and 3.1 percent aged 65 or older.

The population of Tanzania represents 0.67 percent of the world's total population which arguably means that one person in every 151 people on the planet is a resident of Tanzania. This page provides the latest reported value for - Tanzania Population - plus previous releases, historical high and low, short-term forecast and long-term prediction, economic calendar, survey consensus and news. Tanzania Population - actual data, historical chart and calendar of releases - was last updated on December of 2015.

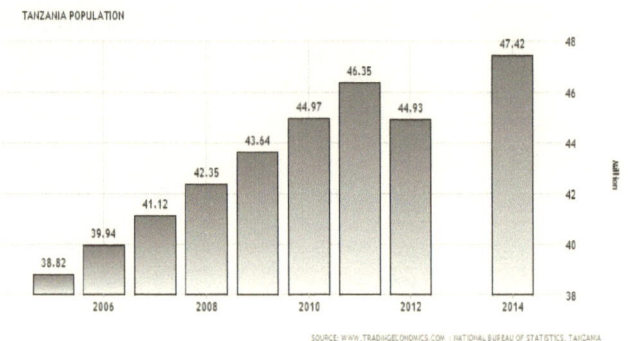

The population distribution in Tanzania is extremely uneven. Most people live on the northern border or the eastern coast, with much of the remainder of the country being sparsely populated. Density varies from 12 per square kilometre (31/sq mi) in the Katavi Region to 3,133 per square kilometre (8,110/sq mi) in the Dar es Salaam Region. Approximately 70 percent of the population is rural, although this percentage has been declining since at least 1967. Dar es Salaamis the *de facto* capital and largest city. Dodoma, located in the centre of Tanzania, is the *de jure* capital, although action to move government buildings to Dodoma has stalled.

The population consists of about 125 ethnic groups. The Sukuma, Nyamwezi, Chagga, and Hayapeoples have more than 1 million members each. Over 100 different languages are spoken in Tanzania, making it the most linguistically diverse country in East Africa. Among the languages spoken in Tanzania are all four of Africa's language families:Bantu, Cushitic, Nilotic, and Khoisan. Swahili and English are Tanzania's official languages. Swahili belongs to the Bantu branch of the Niger-Congo family.

The Sandawe people speak a language that may be related to the Khoe languages of Botswana and Namibia, while the language of the Hadzabe people, although it has similar click consonants, is arguably a language isolate. The language of the Iraqw people is Cushitic. Other languages are Indian languages and Portuguese (spoken by Goans and Mozambicans).

Although much of Zanzibar's native population came from the mainland, one group known as Shiraz is traces its origins to the island's early Persian settlers. Non-Africans residing on the mainland and Zanzibar account for 1 percent of the total population. The Asian community, including Hindus, Sikhs, Shi'a and Sunni Muslims, Parsis, and Goans, has declined by 50 percent in the past decade to 50,000 on the mainland and 4,000 on Zanzibar. An estimated 70,000 Arabs and 20,000 Europeans (90 percent of which are from the British diaspora) reside in Tanzania.

Based on 1999–2003 data, over 74,000 Tanzanian-born people were living in Organization for Economic Co-operation and Development countries, with 32,630 residing in the United Kingdom; 19,960 in Canada; 12,225 in the United States; 1,714 in Australia; 1,180 in the Netherlands; and 1,012 in Sweden.

According to the 2012 census, the total population was 44,928,923 compared to 12,313,469 in 1967, resulting in an annual growth rate of 2.9 percent. The under 15 age group represented 44.1 percent of the population, with 35.5 percent being in the 15–35 age group, 52.2 percent being in the 15–64 age group, and 3.8 percent being older than 64.

According to the 2012 revision of the World Population Prospects, children below the age of 15 constituted 44.8 percent of the total population, with 52.0 percent aged 15–64 and 3.1 percent aged 65 or older.

Structure of the population (01.07.2013) (Estimates):

Age group	Male	Female	Total	Percent
0-14	10 535 389	10 401 745	20 937 134	44,42
15-64	12 078 172	12 726 270	24 804 442	52,63
65+	654 396	736 608	1 391 004	2,95

Births and deaths

Year	Population	Live births	Deaths	Natural increase	Crude birth rate	Crude death rate	Rate of natural increase	TFR
2009		1 667 889	577 393	1 090 496				
2010		1 678 325	573 213	1 105 122				
2011		1 687 203	565 099	1 122 104				
2012	44 928 923	1 694 943	555 975	1 138 968				3.685

MEASURES OF POPULATION STRUCTRE AND GROWTH

1. Dependence Ration

Dependence ratio (DR) = <u>Number of people aged 0-14 + adults 65</u>
Working age group 15 – 64years   x 100

Child dependence ratio = <u>number of people aged 0-14</u> x 100
Number of people aged 15-65

Aged dependence ratio = <u>Number of people aged 65+</u> x 100
Number of people aged 15 64

Positive effects of high dependence ratio:
1. Produce large number of cheap for future working force in the country

2. Leads to the growing market for different manufactured products consumed by the young age e.g. education materials.
3. There little expenditure on luxury demands by the youth.
4. There are little demand for jobs, since the majority are old and young ages
5. Ageing population can result to construction boom in favored retirement location e.g. the *Costa del sol* in Spain
6. There is little rural-urban migration among very young and old group
7. Old people can give abundance advice to the young people according to their experience.
8. Ageing population can lead to a growing "grey" market for leisure and health product for the old
9. Source of employment to the Centre of caring old people.

Negative effects of high dependence ratio
1. Persistent poverty.
2. Burden to tax payers.
3. Increase in burden to the government.
4. Lower pension funds.
5. May leads to the high number of crimes and other social, political and economic evils.

Possible solutions to negative effects of high dependence ratio:
1. Discouragement of high death rate by the use of family planning, so as to reduce age group of 0-14 who are much dependent.
2. Encouragement of money saving to the young people before reaching older age in order to avoid much dependence to the government.
3. Establishment of pensions to the workers; both government and private sectors in order workers to get excess money in their retirement age, so as to reduce much expenses to the government as well as much dependence.

2. Sex Ratio

Sex Ratio = Number of Male in a Given Population   x 100
Number of Females in That Particular Population

3. Birth or Fertility Rate

Crude Birth Rate (CBR) = $\dfrac{\textit{Birth in a Year}}{\textit{Midyear Population}} \times 1000$

General Fertility Rate (GFR) $=$ $\dfrac{\textit{Birth in a Year}}{\textit{Women 15-49 at Midyear}} \times 1000$

Age Specific Fertility Rate (ASFR) = $\dfrac{\textit{Total birth in a year aged}}{\textit{Women aged y at a midyear}} \times 1000$

General marital fertility rate (GMFR) $=$ $\dfrac{\textit{All births in a year}}{\textit{Married women 15-49 years}} \times 1000$

Causes of high birth rate:

1. Poor knowledge and education on family planning.
2. Symbol of prestige in having many children.
3. Sex preferences.
4. Religion factors, as increasing the offspring in the world.
5. Naming of relatives.
6. Considering children as the man power in agricultural activities to the family level.
7. Polygamism in marrying more than one wife.

Positive effects of high birth rate

High birth rate lead to the increase of population, hence the following are advantages:

1. Increase in the numbers of workforce.
2. May lead to the technological development due to high competition in science and technology.
3. Act as the source of markets to different commodities and products.
4. Lead to the increase in production due to high number of workforce.
5. Facilitate to the proper utilization of the available resources.
6. Facilitate to the expansion and improvement of social services in the country.

Negative effects of high birth rate:

1. Leads to the increase of street children.

2. May lead to the increase in dependence ratio.
3. It is the sign for future unemployment.
4. Increase the government expenses in provision of social service.
5. Many children to the family and national level may lead to the decline of living standard in the country hence deaths may occur before reaching the old age.
6. Due to future unemployment, may lead to the increase in crimes and evils.

Solution to the negative effects of high birth rate:
a) Encouragement of late marriage to youths.

b) Provision of family planning education starting at family level up to school level.

c) Formulation of clear population policy that will look to the balance of the available population and development with the available resources.

d) Creation of future employment opportunities.

e) Discouragement of polygamies practices.

f) Discouraging of poor beliefs like naming relatives and sex preference in marriage.

4. Mortality or Dearth rate

Crude death rate (CBR) = $\dfrac{Total\ death\ in\ a\ year}{Midyear\ population}$ x 1000

Age specific death rate (ASDR) = $\dfrac{Total\ number\ of\ deaths\ to\ person\ aged}{Midyear\ population\ to\ person\ aged\ y}$ x1000

Child mortality rate (CMR) = $\dfrac{Number\ of\ deaths\ to\ children < years}{Total\ population\ of\ children < 5years}$ x 1000

Infant mortality rate (IMR) = $\dfrac{Death\ of\ children\ under\ 1\ year}{Live\ births\ in\ a\ given\ year}$ x 1000

Maternal mortality rate (MMR) = $\dfrac{Death\ of\ women}{Total\ births\ in\ a\ year}$ x 100 000

Causes of high mortality or death rate:
 a) Occurrence of wars
 b) Disease like HIV/AIDs and malaria.
 c) Occurrence of accidents.
 d) Strong poverty.
 e) Ignorance in how to take preventive measures in any cause of diseases.
 f) Famine and hunger.
 g) Poor health and medical services.

Effects of high death rate:
 1. Lead to the depopulation.
 2. May influence to the improvement of health services so as to avoid deaths to ill-people.
 3. Decline in number of man power in the country.

Solutions so as to reduce high mortality rate (decline of deaths in the world is due to):
 (a) Prevention of wars.
 (b) Poverty reduction.
 (c) Diseases control.
 (d) Improvement of public health services.
 (e) Improvement of agriculture so as to assure abundance food availability.
 (f) Provision of education on how to people to manage in improving their standard of living.
 (g) Better means of transport.
 (h) Clean and safe water supply.

5. Life expectancy (Life span)

Life expectancy refers to the length of time those living things especially a human being is likely to live. Life span of a human being is termed into high or low life expectancy.

Impact of high life expectance
 1. High dependence ratio due to of high number of old people
 2. Increased number of old people than other age groups
 3. Is the indicator to the country that is develop
 4. Is the symbol of educated and civilize country in all aspects

5. Large number of camps for caring old people.
6. Due to the high number of old people, there is a high government expenses on caring them.
7. Loss of productive workforce due to the large number of old people, hence immigration is required to resolve such problem.
8. Increase in child labor

Impacts of low life expectancy
   o High birth rate to replace the dying people.
   o High number of young people than old people.
   o High mortality rate due to poor living standard and good health care.
   o Much depopulation due to life is being short.

Qn: Discuss for the causes of low and high life span

DEMOGRAPHIC FERTILITY MEASURES
Fertility is measured based on women data. Measures use child births' data. Main measures of fertility are:
1. Child Women Ratio (CWR)

2. Crude Birth Rate (CWR)

3. General Fertility Rate (GFR)

4. Age Specific Fertility Rate (ASFR)

5. Total Fertility Rate (TFR)

6. Gross Reproduction Rate (GRR)

7. Net Reproduction Rate (NRR)

1. Child Women Ratio
It is referred to the ratio of children less than 5 years to women of child bearing. And it is normally expresses per 1, 000 population. In this, fertility is high when child women ratio is high and fertility is low when child women ratio is low. Tend to require basic age-sex data from census; thus easy to calculate.

$$CWR = \frac{Children\ age\ 0-4\ years}{Women\ age\ 15-49\ years} \ x\ 1,000$$

2. Crude Birth Rate

It involves number of births in a year in a community. It is also called birth rate and normally expressed per 1, 000 population. Crude birth rate is a simplest and commonest measure.

$$CBR = \frac{Number\ of\ births\ in\ a\ year}{Mid-year\ population}\ x\ 1,000$$

3. General Fertility Rate

Refers to the number of live births per 1, 000 women aged 15-49 year. It is commonly given as value per thousand. GFR is more refined than CBR since it refers to women at risk of giving births.

$$GFR = \frac{Number\ of\ births}{Number\ of\ women\ ages\ 15-49}\ x\ 1,000$$

4. Age Specific Fertility Rate

This is the number of live births to women of a given age. It is normally expressed per 1, 000 women. ASFR links births and age of mothers.

$$ASFR = \frac{Births\ to\ women\ in\ age\ group\ a}{Female\ population\ age\ group\ a}\ x\ 1,000$$

See the table below of ASFR for Tanzania mainland 1967

Age Group	Women	Births	ASFR	$\%\left(\frac{ASFR}{\Sigma ASFR}\ x\ 100\right)$
15-19	544, 533	91, 836	168.7	11.6
20-24	513, 998	171, 464	334.4	23.0
24-29	543, 729	171, 874	316.1	21.7
30-34	378, 012	98, 152	259.7	17.9
35-39	317, 864	63, 815	200.8	13.8
40-44	219, 540	25, 173	114.7	7.9
45-49	219, 970	13, 176	59.9	4.1
Total	*2, 737, 646*	*635, 490*	*1, 454.3*	*100.0*

By commenting from the table: ASFR shows low contribution of fertility to women in ages 15-19 and above 39 years. Peak is in women aged 20-24 followed by 25-29.

5. Total Fertility Rate

It is the total lifetime number of births a woman will bear. TFR is the sum of ASFR in a single number. TFR shows how many children a woman has. Formula for computing TFR is:

$$TFR = \frac{\Sigma ASFR}{1,000} \; x \; 5 \; or \; \frac{5\Sigma fa}{1,000}$$

Where *fa* is ASFR of age group **a**

6. Reproductive Rates

Reproductive rates have two categories: Gross Reproductive Rate (GRR) and Net Reproductive Rate (NRR).

(a) Gross Reproductive Rate (GRR)

It tends to consider daughters born to a woman in her life time. It is like TFR except, it counts only daughters born. It also Measures women reproducing by having daughters.

(b)Net Reproductive Rate (NRR)

It deals with Daughters born to a woman considering mortality. NRR is usually lower than GRR since it takes into account mortality of women.

Example: GRR and NRR (1993)

COUNTRY	GRR	NRR
Burkina Faso	3.50	2.41
UK	0.80	0.85

From the table, shows that, during her life time a woman in Burkina Faso have 3.5 daughters. In UK a woman have less than one daughter. In Burkina Faso, one daughter would die, before completing her child bearing.

Replacement Level Fertility

It is a level at which women have exactly enough daughters to 'replace' themselves in a population. An NRR of 1.00 is equal to replacement. Today, virtually all developed countries are at or below replacement level fertility.

UK, have an NRR of 0.85 in 1993, is below replacement. TFR can be used to indicate replacement level fertility (through average number of children sufficient to replace both parents. TFR of 2.1 is considered to be replacement level fertility.

Population Momentum

It is the tendency of a population to continue to grow after replacement level fertility has been achieved. A population that has achieved replacement fertility may still continue to grow for some decades. This is because of past high fertility. It leads to a high concentration of people in youngest ages.

DEMOGRAPHIC MORTALITY MEASURES

Mortality refers to the frequency of deaths. Death is defined as a permanent loss of life at any time after a live birth. There are several mortality measures:

a) Crude Death Rate (CDR)

b) Infant Mortality Rate (IMR)

c) Child Mortality Rate (CMR)

d) Under Five Mortality Rate (U5MR)

e) Maternal Mortality Rate (MMR)

f) Life Expectancy

(a) Crude Death Rate (CDR)

It is a simplest and commonest measure of mortality. Refer to number of deaths of a year per 1, 000 population. CBR is represented in a formula as follows:

$$\text{CBR} = \frac{Death\ in\ a\ year}{Mid-year\ population} \times 1,000$$

(b) Infant Mortality Rate (IMR)

Infant Mortality Rate is a mortality of live-born infants who have not reached their first birthday. It is the ratio of deaths of infants under one year during a given year to live births during the same year. Computational formula for IMR is:

$$\text{IMR} = \frac{Deaths\ Under\ age\ 1\ in\ a\ year}{Live\ Births\ in\ a\ year} \times 1,000$$

Infant Mortality Rate is one of sensitive parts of mortality. It is used as an indicator of health conditions and development of a community. It gives chances of dying between birth and first birthday. In Least Developed Countries (LDC), infant mortality is a contributor to deaths.

(c) Under Five Mortality Rate (U5MR)

It is a mortality that occurs to children between ages zero to age five. It is taken because the mortality of under-five differs considerably from adult mortality. Computational formula is:

$$U5MR = \frac{Deaths\ of\ Children\ under\ 5\ years}{Total\ births\ of\ Children\ under\ 5\ years} \times 1,000$$

Usually, under normal conditions there is a higher probability of dying at the age below five year.

(d) Maternal Mortality Rate (MMR)

Maternal Mortality is a widely used cause-specific mortality rate. Maternal Mortality Rate represents risk of dying due to pregnancy complications and child bearing. MMR is expressed as: number of deaths due to puerperal causes per 100, 000. Formula is:

$$MMR = \frac{Deaths\ due\ to\ puerperal\ causes}{Live\ births\ in\ a\ year} \times 100,000$$

Maternal Mortality Rate in developed countries is very low: 10 deaths per 100, 000. And in developing countries it may reach 200 per 100, 000 births.

(e) Life Expectancy (MMR)

Life expectancy is average number of additional years a person could expect to live. It is hypothetical measure because it is based on current death rates. Person's life expectancy changes as one grows older. Life expectancy differs depending on sex and present age.

Life expectancy at birth is most commonly cited life expectancy measure. It is an indicator of current health conditions. Countries with low standard of living often demonstrate a low life expectancy. The following table shows Life Expectancy of selected places (2004).

Area	Life expectancy (years)
Tanzania	45
Rwanda	40
Eastern Africa	46

Middle Africa	50
Southern Africa	62
Northern Africa	67
Western Africa	51
Developing countries	63
Developed countries	76
World	67

AGEING POPULATION

Ageing population refers to the population age in which high number of the population is getting old. Ageing population is caused by the followings:

1. Low fertility rate with high life expectancy.
2. Declined of mortality rate with late marriage and low fertility rate.
3. Child birth spacing due to the increased population with improved health services.

Effect of ageing population:
1. Increased in dependence ratio.
2. Lead to the increase of government expenditure in caring old people.
3. Shortage of workforces due to high number of aged population.
4. High taxes may be directed to the working group who are minority.
5. Changing sectors within the economy due to demand basing to the old people.
6. The government may reduce investment in some sectors due to the lot of funds to be redirected depending to the demand of aging population in the country.

Solution to the effect of ageing population:
1. There should be an increase of participation to the economic development of the country.
2. There should be an addition of time for the retirement rate of workers.
3. The government should search other sources of revenue so as to reduce burdens to the tax payers.
4. There should be mobility of man powers so as to overcome the shortage of workers.

5. People should be educated in how to keep savings for future uses when they get old.
6. There should be an involvement of private sectors in dealing with care of old people.

CHAPTER 17:

SAMPLE QUESTIONS WITH ANSWERS

Qn.1. According to the UN's convention and protocol; a refugee is a person who is outside of his own country and is able or will to return due to a well-founded fear to being persecuted because of race, religion, nationality, membership of a particular group and political opinion. So, what are the factors for the generation of refugees and its possible solution to the problem of refugees in the world? (Give 8 points).

(1) Any relevant definition of refugee(s)

(2) Factors for the generation of refugee:
- *Ethnic and religious conflicts*
- *Environmental disasters*
- *Political violence*
- *Conflict over economic resources*
- *Violation of human rights*

(3) Possible solution to the problem of refugees:
- *Repatriation through returning the country of origin or citizenship*
- *Resettlement in the country of origin*
- *Political integration*
- *Remove ethnic and religion conflict*
- *World should encourage peace and Harmon.*

(4) Any relevant conclusion.

Qn.2. International migrants have been categorized into three: legal migrants, illegal migrants and refugees. Give eight reasons for international migration.

(1) Any relevant definition of migration or international migration.

(2) Reason for the international migration:

- *Economic* like finding work, economic freedom, following career of particular pass.
- *Social* like better quality life, to be close with family or friends, religious factors.
- *Political* reason like instability that caused by civil wars among others
- *Environmental* reason like natural disasters

(3) Any relevant conclusion

Qn. 3. The following are some of the terms associated with demographic information in which you should have to give out their clear meaning:

a) Live birth: *is ability of women to bear a child. Live birth or still birth is called fecundity.*

b) Still birth: *the birth of a dead baby after 24 completed weeks of pregnancy. If the baby dies before 24 completed weeks, it is known as miss carriage or late foetal loss.*

c) Parturition: is the Latin word *"**parturire**"* means "to be ready to bear young". By definition, parturition is the *the act or process of giving birth (chirdbirth) .*

d) Divorce: *it is the situation when a marriage is ended by an official or legal process.*

e) Marriage: *a legally accepted relationship between a woman and a man in which they live as husband and wife, or the official ceremony which results in this.*

f) Foetal (fetal) dearth: *means death prior to the complete expulsion or extraction from its mother of a product of human conception, irrespective of the duration of pregnancy and which is not an induced termination of pregnancy. The death is indicated by the fact that after such expulsion or extraction, the fetus does not breath or show any other evidence of life, such as beating the heart, pulsation of the umbilical cord or definite movement of voluntary muscles.*

The loss of a fetus at any stage is a fetal demise. A death that occurs prior to 20 weeks' gestation is usually classified as a spontaneous abortion; and those occurring after 20 weeks constitute a fetal demise or still birth. If the baby dies before 24 completed weeks, it is known as a miscarriage or late fetal loss.

g) Brain drain (human capital flight): *when large numbers of educated and very skilled people leave their own country to live and work in another one where pay and conditions are better.*

h) Remittance: *is a transfer of money by a foreign worker to an individual in his or her home country. Money sent home by migrants competes with international aid as one of the largest financial inflows to developing countries.*

i) Death: is *the end of life.* Other definition is; death is the cessation of all biological functions that sustain a human being (living organism).

j) Fertility: *the quality of being able to reproduce* **or** *refers to the ability to conceive or to reproduce.*

Qn.4. Why do you think most of new population policies fail within their first five years instead of being formulated well? Vividly, discus the question by citing examples from any country you studied as a case study over population policy (either China or Tanzania).

(1) Any relevant definition and clear introduction of policy and population policy

(2) General factors for the failure (poor implementation) of population policy

(a) For China (One-Child-Policy):

- *Corruption to some government officers*

- *Human right violation, hence china mate with obstacles in this policy*

- *Lack of control in remote areas.*

- *Resisted, because some where not willing to follow the policy implementation.*

- *Birth tourism. Some Chinese arrange tour to other countries so as to have birth.*

- *Hiding and confidentiality to the citizens. They did not report for those went against with the one child policy.*

    (b) For Tanzania (NPP)
- *Poor implementation by the government especially the concerned ministry*
- *Non established and planned institutions*
- *Inadequate recognition of the causal relationship between poverty, population, Environment, genders and development.*
- *Placing more emphasis on meeting demographic targets rather than the need of individuals male and female.*
- *The policies do implement foreign population policies.*
- *Inadequate of human and financial resources*

Qn.5. Write short notes about the following terms:

a) Population dynamic

Population dynamic also can be determined as population change. Population change can be: Change in size, Change in structure, Change in distribution and Change in composition. Components of population change (population dynamics) involve the following: Fertility or Birth, Death or Mortality and Migration (both emigration and immigration). In population dynamic, birth and death are the natural change while migration is the artificial change.

Therefore, *Population change has input output and process (see the model provided below):*

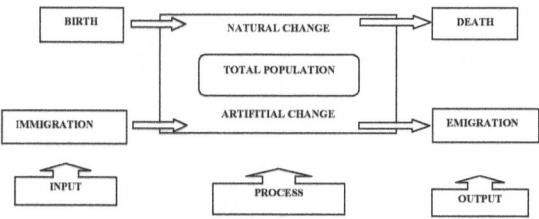

b) Implicit population policy

Implicit Population Policy: refers to the policy, law, regulation or statement which may have direct or indirect effect on population growth. Implicit population policy is not elaborated, as explicit population policy, since it is unclear and cannot be easily understood leading to the failure in terms of implementation.

Implicit Policy have the following traits: The document or statements are not clear Adherences to the statements or regulation are sometime not strict, it may not be a result of pre-existing laws or part of declaration and finally the stipulation of statement is sometime not precise and exact to the point in questions.

c) Population pyramid

Population pyramid is a graphical illustration that shows the distribution of various age groups in a population (typically that of a country or region of the world), which forms the shape of a pyramid when the population is growing. Population pyramid also called as age-sex pyramid, age pyramid or age picture diagram. It is also used in ecology to determine the overall age distribution of a population; an indication of the reproductive capabilities and likelihood of the continuation of a species

Population pyramid has the following characteristics as namely: Shows age's structure of the population, Shows sex structure of the population, Shows the level of development of any country, Shows the level of technology in the country and Shows the relationship between working group and dependent group.

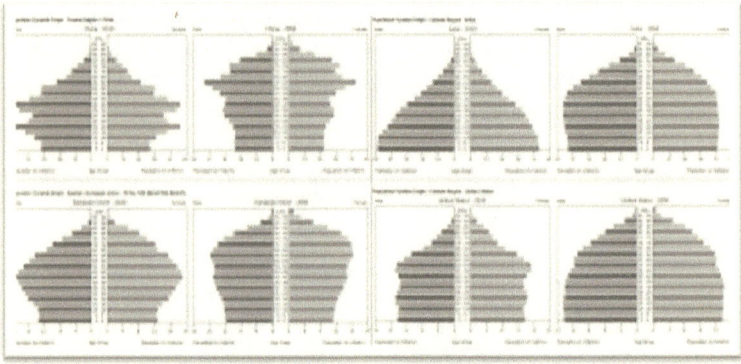

d) Maternal mortality rate

Maternal Mortality Rate (MMR) is a widely used cause-specific mortality rate. Maternal Mortality Rate represents risk of dying due to pregnancy complications and child bearing. MMR is expressed as: number of deaths due to puerperal causes per 100, 000. Formula is:

$$MMR = \frac{Deaths\ due\ to\ puerperal\ causes}{Live\ births\ in\ a\ year} \; x\; 100,000$$

Maternal Mortality Rate in developed countries is very low: 10 deaths per 100, 000. And in developing countries it may reach 200 per 100, 000 births.

e) Life expectancy

Life expectancy is average number of additional years a person could expect to live. It is hypothetical measure because it is based on current death rates. Person's life expectancy changes as one grows older. Life expectancy differs depending on sex and present age.

Life expectancy at birth is most commonly cited life expectancy measure. It is an indicator of current health conditions. Countries with low standard of living often demonstrate a low life expectancy.

Qn.6. Distinguish between each of the following terms:

a) Gross Reproductive Rate from Net Reproductive Rate

Gross Reproductive Rate (GRR) it tends to consider daughters born to a woman in her life time. It is like TFR except, it counts only daughters born. It also Measures women reproducing by having daughters *while* Net Reproductive Rate (NRR) it deals with Daughters born to a woman considering mortality. NRR is usually lower than GRR since it takes into account mortality of women.

b) General Fertility Rate from Total Fertility Rate

General Fertility Rate refers to the number of live births per 1, 000 women aged 15-49 year. It is commonly given as value per thousand. GFR is more refined than CBR since it refers to women at risk of giving births:

$$\text{GFR} = \frac{Number\ of\ births}{Number\ of\ women\ ages\ 15-49} \times 1,000$$

While

Total Fertility Rate It is the total lifetime number of births a woman will bear. TFR is the sum of ASFR in a single number. TFR shows how many children a woman has. Formula for computing TFR is:

$$\text{TFR} = \frac{\Sigma ASFR}{1,000} \times 5 \ or \ \frac{5\Sigma fa}{1,000}$$

c) Sex Ratio from Age Dependency Ratio

Sex ratio is the ratio between males and female in population. Like most sexual reproducing species, the sex ratio in humans 1:1 (this tendency is explained by Fisher's principle). by formulae, sex ratio is:

$$\text{Sex Ratio} = \frac{Number\ of\ Male\ in\ a\ Given\ Population}{Number\ of\ Females\ in\ That\ Particular\ Population} \times 100$$

Dependency ratio is a measure showing the number of dependents, aged zero to 14 and over the age of 65, to the total population, aged 15 t0 64. It is also referred to as the "total dependency ratio". Dependency ratio it is used to measure the pressure on productive population. By formula, dependence ratios are:

$$\text{Dependency ratio (DR)} = \frac{\text{Number of people aged 0-14 + adults 65}}{\text{Working age group 15 – 64 years}} \times 100$$

$$\text{Child dependency ratio} = \frac{\text{Number of people aged 0-14}}{\text{Number of people aged 15-64}} \times 100$$

$$\text{Aged dependency ratio} = \frac{\text{Number of people aged 65+}}{\text{Number of people aged 15-64}} \times 100$$

d) Young Populations from Old Populations

Young population is that population have large proportion of people in the younger age group (below 15) *while* Old population is the same as ageing population. Therefore, ageing or old population refers to the population age in which high number of the population is getting old. Ageing population is caused by the followings: low fertility rate with high life expectancy, declined of mortality rate with late marriage and low fertility rate and child birth spacing due to the increased population with improved health services.

e) Spontaneous abortion from induced abortion

Spontaneous abortion is non-induced embryonic or fetal death or passage of products of conception before 20 weeks of gestation. Miscarriage is also known as spontaneous abortion and pregnancy loss; is the natural death of an embryo or fetus before it is able to survival independently *while* induced abortion is the intentional termination of a pregnancy before the fetus can live independently. An abortion may be elective (based on a women's personal choice) or therapeutic (to preserve the health or save the life of a pregnant woman).

Qn.7. The size of population of Uyui district by the end of the year 1954 was 43, 603. When observing Uyui population between year 1954 and the end of the year 1969, it was discovered that, the number of births were 3, 789, deaths were 4, 500, in-migrant were 600 and out-migrants were 250. Using the above information:

a) Calculate the natural increase

Natural Increase (NI) = Birth – Death

= 3, 7789 – 4, 500

$$NI = -711$$

b) *Calculate the net migration*

Net Migration (NM) = Immigrants – Emigrants

$$= 600 - 250$$
$$NM = 350$$

c) *What was the size of the population by the end of the year 1969?*

$$Pt = Po + (B - D) \pm (I - 0)$$
$$= 43,603 + (3,789 - 4,500) \pm (600 - 250)$$
$$= 43,603 + (-711) \pm (350)$$
$$= 43,603 - 711 + 350$$
$$Pt = 43,242$$

Therefore, population in 1969 was 43,242

d) *Comment on the population of Uyui between 1954 and 1969.*

The population of Uyui between 1954 and 1969 were as:

- Nature increase was negative 711 (means high death rate than birth rates),
- Net migration was 350 (means that, immigrant were very high than emigrants),
- Due to high number of deaths in Uyui, the population tended to decrease in a different of (43,603 – 43,242) 361 from 1954 to 1969.

Qn.8. Carefully, study the births information of Mbakofi village for the year 2009, and then answer the questions given:

Age Group	Both Sexes	Males	Females	Births	ASFR	% $\left(\frac{ASFR}{\Sigma ASFR} \times 100\right)$
15-19	3595735	1761329	1834406	91838		
20-24	3148513	1402077	1746436	153000		
25-29	2801965	1309661	1492304	167909		
30-34	2229046	1087599	1141447	145678		
35-39	1669873	824338	845535	99887		
40-44	1348508	669549	678959	80786		
45-49	984823	478522	506301	765432		
Total	15,778,463	7,533,075	8,245,388	1,504,530		

a) *Calculate the general fertility rate (GFR)*

General Fertility Rate (GFR) = $\frac{\text{Birth of women in a given group at midyear}}{\text{Female population in age 15-49 at midyear}}$ x 1000

$$GFR = \frac{1,504,530}{8,245,388} \; x \; 1000$$

$$\underline{GFR = 182.47}$$

b) *Using the blank columns in the table and provided space below, calculate age specific fertility rate (ASFR)*

By using the blank columns in the table and calculate age specific fertility rate (ASFR). The formula is:

$$ASFR = \frac{Births \; in \; a \; specific \; group}{Female \; population \; in \; specific \; age \; group} \; x \; 1000$$

$$ASFR \; (15\text{-}19) = \frac{91,838}{1,834,406} \; x \; 1000 = 50.06$$

$$ASFR \; (20\text{-}24) = \frac{153,000}{1,746,436} \; x \; 1000 = 87.61$$

$$ASFR \; (25\text{-}29) = \frac{167,909}{1,492,304} \; x \; 1000 = 112.52$$

$$ASFR \; (30\text{-}34) = \frac{145,678}{1,141,447} \; x \; 1000 = 127.63$$

$$ASFR \; (35\text{-}39) = \frac{99,887}{845,535} \; x \; 1000 = 118.13$$

$$ASFR \; (40\text{-}44) = \frac{80,786}{678,959} \; x \; 1000 = 118.99$$

$$ASFR \; (45\text{-}49) = \frac{765,432}{506,301} \; x \; 1000 = 1,511.81$$

Age Group	Both Sexes	Males	Females	Births	ASFR	% $\left(\frac{ASFR}{\Sigma ASFR} \; x \; 100\right)$
15-19	3595735	1761329	1834406	91838	50.06	
20-24	3148513	1402077	1746436	153000	87.61	
25-29	2801965	1309661	1492304	167909	112.52	
30-34	2229046	1087599	1141447	145678	127.63	
35-39	1669873	824338	845535	99887	118.13	
40-44	1348508	669549	678959	80786	118.99	
45-49	984823	478522	506301	765432	1511.81	
Total	15,778,463	7,533,075	8,245,388	1,504,530	2,126.55	

c) *Calculate the total fertility rate (TFR)*

$$TFR = \frac{\Sigma ASFR}{1,000} \; x \; 5 \; or \; \frac{5\Sigma fa}{1,000}$$

Where fa is ASFR of age group **a**

$$TFR = \frac{5\sum ASFR}{1000} = \frac{5 \times 2126.55}{1000} = 10.63$$

Therefore, TFR = 10.63

d) Given the sex ratio at birth of 1.05 in Mbakofi village, calculate the general reproductive rate (GRR).

GRR = TFR x Sex Ratio at birth

Thus, GRR = 10.63 x 1.05

$$GRR = 10.63 \times \frac{105}{100}$$

$$= 10.63 \times 1.05$$

$$= 11.1615$$

Therefore, GRR = TFR x Proportional rate

$$TFR \times \frac{f}{m+f} = 10.63 \times \frac{105}{100+105}$$

$$= 10.63 \times 0.512$$

GRR = 5.44.

TRIAL QUESTIONS

1. The world's population is very rapidly;

(a) What are the main reasons for the rapid growth?

(b) How can the population explosion be restrained?

2. It is true to say that "the power of population is indefinitely greater than the power of the earth to produce substance for man?"

3. Describe and account for the main features of population distribution in the world today.

4. How is the population structure of a country affected by;

    a. The standard of living

    b. The infant mortality rate

    c. Migration

    d. Life expectance rate?

5. What are the major problems of either overpopulated or under-populated countries? With reference to any one country, show how such problem can be alleviated

6. What are the major reasons which prompt large scale international migration? Show how these have affected the movement of population to either Tanzania or Nigeria?

7. "Migration alone can never solve the unbalance distribution of world population. Discuss

8. What problems are encountered in providing satisfactory means of employment in densely populated country with rapidly growing population?

9. Discuss the part played by climate in the distribution of mankind

10. How far is it true to say that metropolitan areas generate their own population problems?

11. With reference to either china or Nigeria, describe the pattern of population distribution. In what ways is an unbalanced distribution of population as difficult a problem as over population or under population?

12. Assess the factors that have contributed to the rapid growth of population in many African nations

13. Migration only assumed international important during the 19th and early 20th centuries. Why was earlier migration restricted and why is migration is less important today?

14. Write short notes on the following:

   a. Crude birth rate

   b. Ageing population

   c. The effect of wars on population structure

   d. Internal population movements

15. "A rapid growing population may be asset or hability" discuss this statement and illustrate with reference to; a densely populated rural areas in the tropics, and a highly urbanized temperate industrial areas.

16. Outline the reasons for the migration of population to the towns in any one region you have studied and discuss the problems associated with a rapid increase of population in the cities and in the country side

17. With reference of any one country you have studied, show how the distribution of population is related to the distribution of economic activities.

18. Describe and attempt to the patterns of internal migration to be found in any one country you have studied

19. Either describe and attempt to explain the movement of population to the towns in any country which you have studied. Or describe what is meant by the term "urban hierarchy" of any two countries which you have studied

20. With the help of a sketch map, outline and comment on the distribution of urban and rural in Tanzania. Why some areas are more densely populated than others.

21. In what ways do the population problems of developed countries differ from those of developing countries?

22. "Too many people on too little land" To what extent is this a satisfactory statement about over population

23. With vivid examples, discuss the impact of rapid population growth on urban and rural areas.

24. With reference to examples, discuss the reason for, and the results of international migrations of population

25. Why do large scale international migrations of population occurs? What problems have arisen as a result of such international migrations?

CHAPTER 18:

POPULATION SETTLEMENT

The study of settlement is basic to human geography because the form of settlement in any particular region reflects man's relationship with environment. Settlement reflects not only man's response to his environment but also the religion and social customs of his society. Some buildings in town or village are always reserved for public use, such as town or village hall, a church, mosque, or temple, administrative buildings or the place of a local rulers. The type and number of such buildings help to give settlements their distinctiveness.

Similarly in settlements where several different groups of people are different groups of people are thrown together, the town or village may be divided into separate quarters; each distinguished by particular building styles or house arrangement or by different religions or other communal buildings. In fact the almost endless variety of settlements can be classified in several different ways. The most obvious division is into *towns and villages*. Also settlements can be classified by their *patterns* or *shapes* like *dispersed, nucleated*, *linear*, and *star shaped*.

Definition of Concepts

Site refers to the actual piece of ground on which settlement is built. Situation or position refers to the location of the village or town in relation to the surrounding areas. In turn, the site or situations of settlements are often determined by their *function*. Settlement is the place where people live together. Or, is the place with housing units where group of people live together.

Types of Settlement

There are two main types of settlement, namely:
   (a) Urban or town settlement.
   (b) Rural or village settlement.

A. Urban Settlement

Urban settlement is the settlement area made up by towns, centers, cities (made up by township areas).

Characteristics of urban settlement:
   (1) Economic activities are non-agriculture activities.
   (2) Continuous building.

(3) High density in of population.
(4) Nucleated in settlement patterns.

B. Rural Settlement
Rural settlement is the type of settlement that found in rural areas. Settlement is in homestead.

Characteristics of Rural settlement:
(1) Occupation is located at homestead that make people their homes
(2) The major economic activity is agriculture.
(3) Low population
(4) Scattered settlement

Settlement Patterns (rural settlement patterns)
Settlement patterns depend on size of settlement, patterns and shape of the settlement. The type of the settlement pattern is determined by the following factors:
(a) Size of the population.
(b) Size of the village or center.
(c) Stage of development of the village or center.
(d) Number of people.

Categories of settlement pattern
Settlement patterns are categorized into three namely:
(a) Linear settlement patterns.
(b) Scattered settlement patterns.
(c) Nucleated settlement patterns.

Scattered Settlement Pattern
Scattered settlement pattern it is also known as *sparse settlement patterns*. In this, dwellings are randomly spread out over areas. It is commonly found in rural areas, where lands are free.

Characteristics of scattered pattern:
i.   Home steady are generally isolated.
ii. Agriculture is the main economic activities.
iii. Have poor infrastructures.
iv. Population size and density is low.

Nucleated Settlement Pattern

It is also known as clustered or compact settlement patterns. Dwelling and other buildings are concentrated in a group of a small area. The pattern indicates high density of settlement. Nucleated settlements are found in urban areas such as towns and cities. Nucleated settlement develops because of the following reasons:

(a) Availability of social services like hospital and school.
(b) Presence of natural and industries.
(c) Presence of natural resources, such as minerals or water.
(d) Limitation of land for building.
(e) Presence of security
(f) Availability of trade and commerce.

Characteristics of Nucleated settlement:
(i)   Home steeds are generally close together.
(ii)   Presence of trade and commerce.
(iii)   Availability of social services.
(iv)   Presence of transport and communication system.
(v)   Characterized by high population density.

Linear Settlement Patterns
It is the settlement pattern where buildings are developed along specific features like rivers, roads, beaches and railways. Buildings are arranged in line following the course of the features.

A linear settlement pattern is influenced by the following factors:
(i)   Presence of river that may be a source of water for people.
(ii)   Presence of road or railway which is a means of transport.
(iii)   Presence of a coast line or shore along which fishermen do their fishing.
(iv)   Suitable terrain that having fertility soil for cultivation e.g. on the food of an escapement.

Characteristics of linear settlement patterns:
(1) Home steady are generally isolated.
(2) Population density is moderate.
(3) Buildings are in a line along the features.

Function of Settlements
Function of settlements refers to activities and services provided in a given settlements for example agriculture, mining, fishing among others.

The major functions of towns are trade, transport, resource extraction, industrial production, defiance, administration, culture and recreation. Towns may more than one function and it is then said to be *diversified* in function.

When settlement has certain service or is a host to certain activities, it is described by using terms like agricultural centers, Administrative centers, market centers mentioning by few.

Forms of Settlement

Instead of settlements patterns, there are also forms of settlements. Therefore, settlements have the following forms:

Circular Rural Settlements: The circular form consists of a central open space surrounded by structures. This model has a center with homes, barns, schools, and churches and as you move away from the center, it is surrounded by farmland.

Linear Rural Settlements: Linear rural settlements feature, buildings clustered along a road, river, or dike to facilitate communications. The fields extend behind the buildings in long, narrow strips. The town would follow the river.

Rectangular: Settlements grow in block due to industrialization, commercial, recreational, administrative, and dwellings.

T-forms: are t-shaped forms of settlements.

Cross-forms: plus-sign-like forms of settlement

Settlement Hierarchy

Settlement hierarchy refers to the way of arranging settlements into a hierarchy based upon their population or some other criteria. Settlements in order of size are in the following:

Megalopolis: Where conurbations have joined to become one large urban area. 10 million and above people. *Conurbation:* A group of large cities and their suburbs that have strong links connecting them to each other. 3-10 million people. *Metropolis:* A city and surrounding towns that is in close proximity and has started to merge into each other. 1-3 million people.

Large city: A city with a large population and many services. 300,000 - 1 million people. *City:* A city would have a wide range of services but not as many as a large city. 100, 000-300, 000 people. *Large Town:* Large towns now see a much more varied range of shops available when compared to villages. 20, 000-100, 000 people. *Town:* Towns see an increase in services, for example, they would have senior schools and police stations. 1, 000-20, 000 people.

Village: Villages start to have some basic services like a petrol station or a village shop: 100 - 1, 000 people. *Hamlet:* Hamlets have very tiny populations and few services, if any and it's less 100 people. *Isolated Dwelling:* Isolated dwelling often in rural areas, these tend to be farmhouses or holiday homes. It has few buildings at most.

Function of Settlement

The function of a settlement is what the people who lived and worked in the settlement did or do. Consider what the settlement is mainly used for. Settlements often have more than one function and the function of most settlements change through time. These are;

Tourist centers: In these areas many jobs and services are related to tourism. Tourists visit this area for its scenery, leisure activities and attractions. Facilities and accommodation have to be provided for these visiting tourists.

Industrial function: In these cities there are a lot of factories and warehouses. Traditionally industrial premises would have been in the middle of the settlements but now they tend to be based on industrial estates.

A centre of local government: A centre of government settlement contains local or national government buildings. This is where there are a lot of jobs related to the administration of the region or country.

A residential settlement: Residential or dormitory settlements have lots of houses but few services. They are often found near larger settlements that provide a good range of jobs and amenities. People will often live in these settlements but work elsewhere. This is called commuting.

A market town: This is where the weekly or monthly market held. Farmers would travel from the surrounding area to sell goods, livestock and produce. Many rural towns still hold markets, but many of these have moved to premises in the town's outskirts.

Port and Harbour: Port and harbour settlements are found along the coast and are sited at points where ships and boats can dock. Whereas larger ports, sited on deep inlets used by ships for the import and export of goods or the transport of people.

Natural Resources: Natural resources in the area enabled Kahama and Mwadui to develop as an important centre in the gold and Tanzanite mining.

Protection: One of the main benefits of living near other people is protection from predators like lions. Living near many other people increased the chances of survival.

A Holiday Resort: Have lots of attractions and shops for tourists to visit and relax in.

Importance of Settlements

A well-established settlement has the following importance:

(1) *Availability of social services.* Settlements make people to be together hence enabling the government and NGOs to provide social services.

(2) *Enhance security.* When people are organized in a settlement, defense and to be easily and smoothly conducted.

(3) *Economic development.* When citizens are settled in a group make easier for diffusion of economic development (e.g. Banks, industries etc.)

(4) *Political services.* When people live together it makes easier for them to participate in different economic activities.

Growth of Settlements (factors encouraging settlement)

Factors influencing the growth of settlements can be categorized into two factors that in one way or another can influence (encourage) or discourage settlements due to the absence or presence of them in an area:

(i)   Human factors.

(ii)   Physical factors.

Physical Factors:
- (a) Climate
    - * Temperature.
    - * Rainfall.
- (b) Soil or edaphic.
- (c) Topography/relief.
- (d) Drainage (Water).
- (e) Natural resources.
- (f) Vegetation.
- (g) Pest and diseases.

Human Factors:
- (a) Historical factors.
- (b) Political factors.
- (c) Economic factors.
- (d) Cultural factors.

Urbanization

Urbanization refers to the process in increase of population in an area to become a town. Urbanization sometimes defined as the process by which more and more people leave the countryside to live in town or cities. *Urbanize* is to build houses, offices, etc. in an area of a countryside so that to become a town. *Overcrowding in urban* refers to the high concentration of population in urban areas.

Advantages of urbanization (overcrowding in urban areas):
1. Influence import and export of products.
2. Facilitate foreign investments.
3. Facilitate manufacturing activities.
4. Influence cultural change.
5. Foster for intermarriage.
6. Led for the rise of centre for social services.
7. Led to the development of administrative centre.

Problems of (Urbanization) overcrowding in urban areas:
1. Under production.
2. Environmental pollution and degradation.
3. Stratification.

4. High concentrated buildings.
5. Shortage of social services.
6. Destruction of culture and moral decay.
7. Increase of evils and crimes.

Solution to the overcrowding in urban areas:
1. Practice of family planning.
2. Control of rural urban migration
3. Decentralization.
4. Establishments of open spaces.
5. Clear plan of infrastructure.
6. Redistribution of people.
7. Opening and establishing new resident areas.
8. Formulation and enforcement of laws that might protect urban and cities.

Social and Economic Problems Associated With Urban Growth:

Better settlements in rural and urban areas go hand in hand with socio-economic development and their consequents or problems. The following are some of the problems associated with urban growth:

(a) Environmental degradation.
(b) Traffic congestion.
(c) Unemployment.
(d) Increase in number of street children.
(e) Immorality (moral decay).
(f) Poor and shortage of social services.
(g) Increase of crime and evils.

Solutions to the Problems Related To Urban Growth:

(1) Application of family planning: There should be and emphasize of family planning to the people, so as to avoid high birth rate that leads to the high number of population to the urban areas.

(2) Establishment of reliable transport: Availability of many transports may avoid problems to the traffic conjugation in urban areas.

(3) Improvement of provision of water services: Water supply should be enough of water to the population in urban areas.

(4) Government policies: There should be clear policies that imposed by the government which discourage high number of immigrants.

(5) Development of informal sectors: There should be promotion of informal sectors that will provide employment opportunities and loans to the urban population so as to avoid the high rate of unemployed people and beggars in urban centers.

(6) Improvement of rural settlements: The government should also improve the rural settlements by providing equal distribution of social services like water supply, schools, health services and transport system between urban and rural area. Equal distribution of social services may lead to the decline of rural-urban migration; hence the population of urban areas will not grow to the maximum.

TRIAL QUESTIONS

(1) Distinguish between urban and rural settlement.

(2) Discuss seven social and economic problems associated with urban growth and suggest possible solutions.

(3) Describe the following settlement patterns:

  (a) Linear.

  (b) Nucleated.

  (c) Scattered.

(4) Explain how the following factors may influence growth of settlements:

  (a) Human factors.

  (b) Physical factors.

(5) With vivid examples, highlight for the factors influencing the distribution of Settlement.

(6) What are the main siting factors of settlement? Show how the site of rural settlements may hinder or encourage their growth.

(7) With reference to any two of the following function affects the appearance and morphology of towns:

  (a) Administration.

  (b) Industrial production.

(c) Defiance.

(d) Trade.

(8) Describe the effects of economic factors on the internal zoning of town. What other factors can cause urban zoning?

(9) Why are towns constantly growing both in population and in area? What are the major problems by urban growth?

(10) Analyze how geographical conditions have contributed to the growth of dense populations to the township areas.

(10) What are the chief factors leading to the development of nucleated and dispersed settlement patterns?

(12) Why are the large cities today of relatively recent development? Describe the growth of any two of them in Tanzania.

(13) Analyze the nature of the large town of your own country. How was each of them founded? And what factors have caused their recent growth or decline?

(14) In what ways may the function of small towns reflect the activities of the surrounding country side?

CHAPTER 19:

POPULATION AND ENVIRONMENT

Environment is all external conditions surrounding an organism and which have influence over its behavior or activities. Environment is also referred to all things that surrounding human being. Environment is classified into the following three:

(a) The past environment.
(b) The current environment.
(c) The future environment.

The Past Environment: it is the sum of all external conditions surroundings the human being after the current environment. This gives to the organisms, which are seen today. *The Current Environment:* Are all external conditions surrounding the organism currently. It moulds the organism of tomorrow. *The Future Environment:* Is the sum of all external conditions expedited to surround the organism in future. This mould the organism after their passage through the two previous named environment.

Components of Environment

There are two components of environment, namely, the living components and the non-living component.

The Living Components: This is also known as Biological environment that include all living organism and macro-organism i.e. plants animal, people, microorganism and macro-organism. *The Non-Living Components:* This include gases, liquids and solids also it includes; Atmospheric environment, Hydrological environment and whole this environment.

Importance of Environment

The followings are various ways in which the environment is important:

(1) *Environment sustains life.* Environment support life to the living things because it provides water, soil food and place for settlement as well as air.

(2) *Environment provides natural resources.* All natural resources are obtained from the environment. Examples of natural resources are forest, soil, water

minerals etc. These natural resources area very importance for economic development.

(3) *Environment has aesthetic values.* Aesthetic value are demographically landscape drainage, feature, Low land fauna are the beautiful to look at the natural settings. These features can act as the source of economic development.

Qn. What is the social-economic importance of environment? (Give 8 points)

Environmental Problems

Environmental problems referred as the hazards or risks. Hazard referred as danger or risks. Environmental problems are potential up several calamities or disasters. There is a relationship between environmental hazards and human activities. The following are the common environmental problems:

(1) Loss of biodiversity.   (7) Epidemics.
(2) Soil erosion.   (8) Pollution.
(3) Diseases.   (9) Drought.
(4) Over grazing.   (10) Desertification.
(5) Over population.   (11) Harmful radiation.
(6) Over cultivation.   (12) Global warming.

1. Loss of Biodiversity

Biodiversity is the variety of species of organism on the earth. The process of loss of biodiversity is called *extinction.* Loss of biodiversity refers to the disappearance of different organism both fauna and flora. Loss of biodiversity is generally caused by deforestation, burning forest, natural disaster, mining, use of harmful chemicals among others. The causes can be either natural or human as shown below:

(a) Natural causes:
   (1) *Occurrence of floods*: Floods kill most kind of organisms at the place where they occurs.
   (2) *Natural lightning*: Natural electricity also cause to the loss of biodiversity like plant and animals.
   (3) *Wind storms:* Excessive winds (strong wind) uproot plants and cause massive death of plant and animal.
   (4) *Pests and diseases*: High rate of pests and diseases tend to kill large number of organisms.

(5) *Land slide:* This kind of mass movement also lead to the loss of biodiversity on the earth.

(6) *Earth quake, Eruption of volcanism, Gravitation etc.* also the cases of loss of biodiversity on the earth in their occurrence.

(b) Human causes:

These are human activities which cause for loss of biodiversity. The following are some of human causes for loss of biodiversity:

(1) *The use of bombs in the war:* The use of bombs in the war leads to the loss or killing of many people and other biodiversity hence loss of biodiversity.

(2) *Pollution*: Both water, air, and land pollution causes for loss of biodiversity. Pollution refers to the addition of wastes or unwanted material on the land, water and air (Environment).

(3) *Bad fishing method:* Unlawful fishing in the water bodies also led to the loss of biodiversity due to the excessive extraction of aquatic materials in the water and the uses of poisons and other bad methods of fishing.

(4) *Bad methods of cultivation:* Poor methods of cultivation like the use of fertilizers, shifting cultivation also may cause to the loss of biodiversity.

(5) *Soil erosion:* Soil erosion that influenced by different erosive agents, also cause for the massive loss of biodiversity to the environment.

(6) *Over population*: Overpopulation that associated with establishment of settlements and different human activities in one way or another cause for the loss of biodiversity.

(7) *Desertification:* Excessive destruction of trees and other vegetation cover tend to cause for the loss of biodiversity, especially those depends their lives on vegetation.

The Effects of Loss of Biodiversity:

(1) Lead to the failure of ecology and scientific activities.

(2) Decrease of living organism.

(3) Lead to the depreciations in aesthetic value of the environment.

2. Environmental Pollution

It is the process of additional of harmful materials into the environment. Environmental pollution is in term of; air, water, land, and noise. Pollution can be in state of gases, liquid, or solid.

Forms of Pollution:
  (d) Water pollution.
  (e) Air pollution.
  (f) Noise pollution (sound waves).
  (g) Land or soil pollution.

A. Water Pollution

Water pollution refers to the addition of unwanted harmful substances (materials) in the water sources. Water pollution is caused by some of the following:

  (1) Disposal of oil, wastes and other products.
  (2) Disposal of sewage materials from homes.
  (3) Fertilizers from agricultural activities.
  (4) Bad methods of fishing like the uses of poison.
  (5) Water transportation that mostly lead to oil spillover.
  (6) Irrigation agriculture that taking place near the sources of water.

Effects of Water Pollution:
  (i) Lead to the loss of biodiversity.
  (ii) Facilitate to air pollution due to bad smell of water.
  (iii) Cause for acidic rainfall.
  (iv) May lead for inadequate of clean and safe water.

Possible Solution to the Effects of Water Pollution:
  (1) To avoid bad methods of agriculture like the use of chemicals in irrigation schemes nearby source of water.
  (2) There should be an establishment of laws to protect the sources of water.
  (3) Ships should be checked before starting their journey so as to avoid the problems of oil spill over.
  (4) People should avoid bad method of fishing, especially in the use of poisons.
  (5) Education should be given to the people so as to avoid pollution of water sources.

B. Air Pollution

Air pollution refers to the addition of harmful substance in the air (atmosphere). The following are some of the causes of air pollution:

(1) *Exhaust smoke from industries*, which tend to contaminate with atmospheric air.

(2) *Car fumes.* These are smokes from different motor vehicles that also can cause for the pollution of air.

(3) *Volcanic eruptions.* In all of volcanic eruption led to the emission of harmful chemical gases that tend to be contaminated to the atmospheric air (gas). Most of gases came from volcanic eruption contain sulphur gases and carbon dioxide.

(4) *Dusts from windstorms.* Different dusts caused by wind storms also tend to pollute the atmospheric air hence air pollution can take place.

(5) *Mining and Quarrying activities.* Mining and quarrying activities contribute to the air pollution through the use of exploitive materials. Also mining and quarrying machines and chemical used in the mineral processing tend to pollute the air.

(6) *Uses of chemical sprays.* This is through poisonous gases and liquid are released into the atmosphere from factories, farms (agricultural activities).

(7) *Bush fire.* Setting fire in the forest and bushes for clearing the area so as to be used in agricultural activities, construction of industries and establishment of settlements also cause for the additional of carbon dioxide and other harmful gases in the atmosphere, hence air pollution may occur.

Effects of Air Pollution
The following are the effects caused by air pollution:
   (i) Loss of biodiversity.
   (ii) Decline of oxygen gas.
   (iii) Depletion of ozone layer.
   (iv) Led to the Global warming.
   (v) May led to the formation of acidic rain.
   (iv) Eruption of air bone deceases.

Solution to the Effects of Air Pollution
The following are the ways to be used or under taken so as to stop the prolonged effects of air pollution:

(1) Provision of environmental education so as to avoid air pollution

(2) Enforcement of laws that prohibit air pollution.

(3) Formulations of environmental policies that emphasizes on environmental protection.

(4) Prohibition in the use of chemical sprays in any economic activities.

(5) To avoid and discourage bush firing.

(6) Afforestation and reforestation that may promote to the increase of vegetation cover that may trap all harmful gases both from mining and industries.

C. Noise Pollution

Noise pollution is the addition of different noises on the environment noise pollutions are caused through the following:

(i) High pitch and booming music.
(ii) Noises from motor vehicles.
(iv) Noises of machine from factories and machine from construction sites.
(vi) Noises through bombs from military operations and practices.
(vii) Noises from explosive methods in quarrying and mining activities.

Effects of Noise Pollution:
(1) Led to communication barrier.
(2) May cause for ear problems.
(3) Led to the mental problems.
(4) May lead to the headache.

Solution to the Effects of Noise Pollution
The following are the major ways of overcoming the noise pollution:
(i) There should be a frequent health checkup.
(ii) There should be a reduction of noises in the environment.
(iii) There should be an alternative source of power in the factory instead of using generators.

Qn. *Describes the causes, mismanagement and effects of pollution with suggestive solutions to the effects.*

3. Land or Soil Degradation (environmental degradation)

This refers to the destruction of soil or land surface. This is caused by big construction activities, poor cultivation methods, overgrazing, mining activities and soil erosion.

4. Deforestation

Deforestation is the disappearance of trees. This is caused by poor cultivation methods, overgrazing, lumbering, construction, needs for fuel wood, charcoal and rapid population growth.

5. Global Warming

It is the gradual increase in temperature on the earth's surface. This is caused by emission of harmful gases (methane, hydrocarbon, NO_2, CO_2), which present the heat energy from escaping in the space in the world. People add 6 billion tons of CO_2 annually by 3 billion tones are absorbed by ocean and plants. Chlorofluorocarbons (CFCS).

6. Natural Hazards

Natural hazards are like, drought, flood among others.

7. Desertification

Desertification is the sum of all process on the environment which results in the formation of desert; it is simply the development of desert. Desertification is caused by natural and human factors, which they include, the followings:

(i) *Insufficient rainfall*. Absence or low rainfall in an area may give the chance for desertification.

(ii) *High temperature*. High temperature lead to the high rate of evaporation, hence may lead to the drought in an area leading to the (desertification) dry of vegetation.

(iii) *Cold ocean currents*. Cold Ocean currents they drop moist over the sea and reach the land as dry wind, hence may lead to the desertification on the area.

(iv) *Relief barrier*. Land situated on the leeward sides on mountain ranges may become a desert because of the rain shadow effect on the mountain. Wind ward sides receive rainfall unlike to leeward side that may influence to the desertification.

(v) *Vast distance from the sea*. The land located far away from the sea or ocean that may have low or no rainfall. These places located away from the sea may become deserts because of lacking moist wind from the sea or ocean.

(vi) ***Dry wind system.*** The wind originated from the interior of continents can lead to the desertification of region over which they blow.

(vii) ***High pressure system.*** Areas that have high pressure system with low humidity, there is no rainfall in those areas, hence desertification.

(viii) ***Human activities.*** Human activities also may influence desertification. The human activities are like:

    a. Bad method of agriculture that practiced through:

          ○ Monoculture.

          ○ Shifting cultivation.

          ○ High use of inorganic fertilizers.

    b. Animal keeping with over grazing.

    c. Deforestation; that influenced by cutting trees for different uses like firewood, timber, charcoal also lead to the desertification.

    d. Bush fires. The process of burning forests and bushes also tend to cause desertification.

The environmental problems are caused by the following environmental hazards:

(1) Floods.	(5) Earth quakes.
(2) Lighting.	(6) Volcanic eruption.
(3) Pest and diseases.	(7) Nuclear wastes.
(4) Drought.	(8) Wind storms.

Note: Some geographers do consider hazards to be actual problems.

CHAPTER 20:

POPULATION PROBLEMS

Population problems are those challenges caused by population. Population problems are caused by the presence of population in association with population characteristics. The size, structure and distribution of population in the country must be viewed in relation to the country's natural resources, technology and technique of production used by the people.

Population problems is determined by the over population and under population in relation to the utilization of resources. If the country has optimum population it means that, there is a balance between population and the available resources. Population problems are associated with population growth. A growing population can be an asset or a liability (burden). Therefore, the following are the negative effects of population growth that exposes population problems:

(1) *Creates pressure on scarce resources:* high population pressure leads to the over exploitation (utilization) on the available resources, hence exhaustion of resources.

(2) *Increase in the rate of unemployment:* high population cause for unemployment because of the presence of large number of population on the particular area or country.

(3) *Increase of environmental problems:* presence of large number of population may cause for the environmental pollution and degradation on the area.

(4) *Increase in the number of beggars*: high population may cause for the increase of beggars especially in urban areas like Mwanza, Dodoma and Dar es Salaam in tanzania.

(5) *Led to the shortage of social services:* The population increase may lead to the shortage of social services in the fact that, the provided social services may not accommodate the increased population. Examples of social services are school, Hospital, Water supply.

(6) *Increase government expenditure:* The government budget may increase due to the increase of population.

On: Suggest with examples for the positive effect of population growth by using any country from East Africa.

Possible Solution to the Population Problem:
   (a) Introduction of family planning: This method may avoid to the high birth rate, hence solution to the population problems.

   (b) Improvement in provision of social services: Both in rural and urban areas, social services should be improved so as to avoid the shortage of social services to the increased population.

   (c) Creation of employment opportunities: There should be an improvement of agricultural sector so as people to employ themselves in the sector in order to solve the problem of an employment to the increased population.

   (d) Introduction of environmental policy: Enactment of environmental policy may facilitate in validation of environmental pollution and degradation.

   (e) There should be minimization of dependence ratio in the country: The number of beggars should be reduced by creating employment opportunities.

BIBLIOGRAPHY

Hill K, Lopez AD et al (2007). Interim measures for meeting needs for health sector data: births, deaths and causes of death. Lancet **370**(9599): 1726-1735.

Kolars, J. and Nyastuen, J.D, (1974). Human Geography: spatial design in World society, New York: McGraw-Hill.

Mahapatra P, Shibuya K, Lopez AD, Coullare F, Notzon FC, Rao C, Szreter (2007). Civil registration systems and vital statistics: successes and missed opportunities. Lancet **370** (9599): 1653-1663.

Msabila, D.T, (2003). An integrated Regional Study On Human economic Geography, Dar es Salaaam: NyambariNyangwine Publishers.

National Population Policy (NPP). (1992). United Republic of Tanzania

National Population Policy (NPP). (2006). United Republic of Tanzania

Philemon Frank. (2016). Human population and Development: http://www.com (kindle direct; accessed March 28, 2016).

Selzer W, Anderson M, (2001). The dark side of numbers: The role of population data systems in human rights abuses. Social Research **68**(2):481-513.

Setel PW, Macfarlane SB, Szreter S, Mikkelsen L, Jha P, Stout S, AbouZahr C (2007). A scandal of invisibility: making everyone count by counting everyone. Lancet **370**(9599): 1569-1577.

United Nations (2001). Principles and Recommendations for a Vital Statistics System: Revision 2. New York: Department of Economic and Social Affairs. Available at: http://unstats.un.org/unsd/pubs/gesgrid.asp?id=264 [Accessed 5th December 2015].

United Nations (2008). Principles and Recommendations for Population and Housing Censuses v.2. New York: Department of Economic and Social Affairs. Available at:http://unstats.un.org/unsd/publication/SeriesM/Seriesm_67rev2e.pdf [Accessed 8th January 2016].

United Nations Economic Commission for Europe. (2007). Register-based statistics in Nordic countries: Review of best practices with focus on population and social statistics. New York and Geneva: United Nations. Available at: http://www.unece.org/fileadmin/DAM/stats/publications/Register_based_statistics_in_Nordic_countries.pdf [Accessed 8th January 2016].